84 Portraits
in Chiaroscuro

Philippe FLOHIC

Welcome to the captivating world of chiaroscuro portrait!

This book presents a selection of 84 portraits created by the author, highlighting this striking artistic technique.

With exceptional mastery of the contrast between light and dark areas, each captivating portrait will take you on a journey into a world of nuances and depths.

The represented faces, each with their own personality and story, showcase the extent of the author's creativity and talent.

With this book, you will discover how chiaroscuro can transform a simple portrait into a striking and timeless work of art.

Whether you are an art enthusiast or a budding artist, you will be inspired by these striking portraits that will allow you to discover the art of chiaroscuro in a new light.

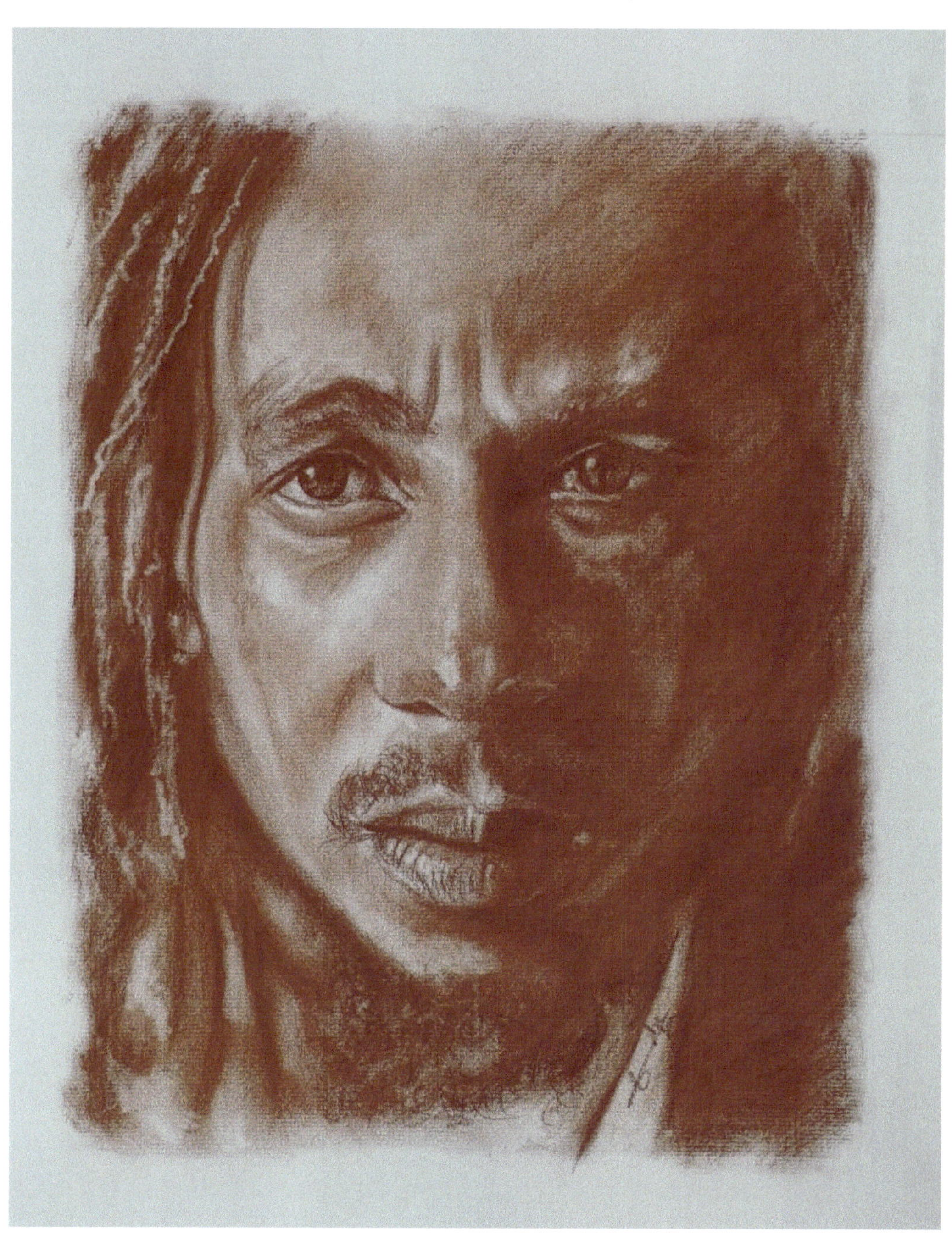

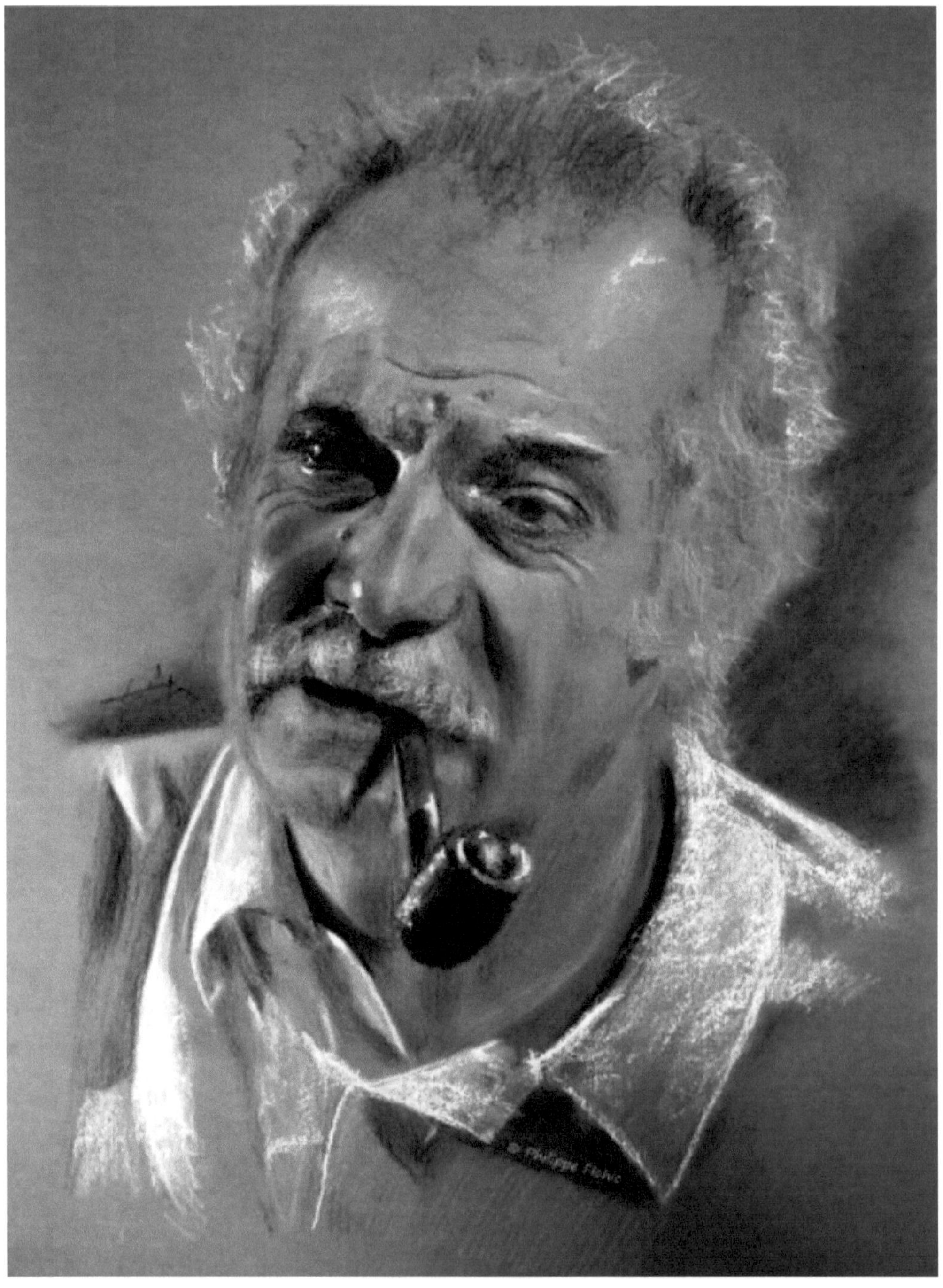

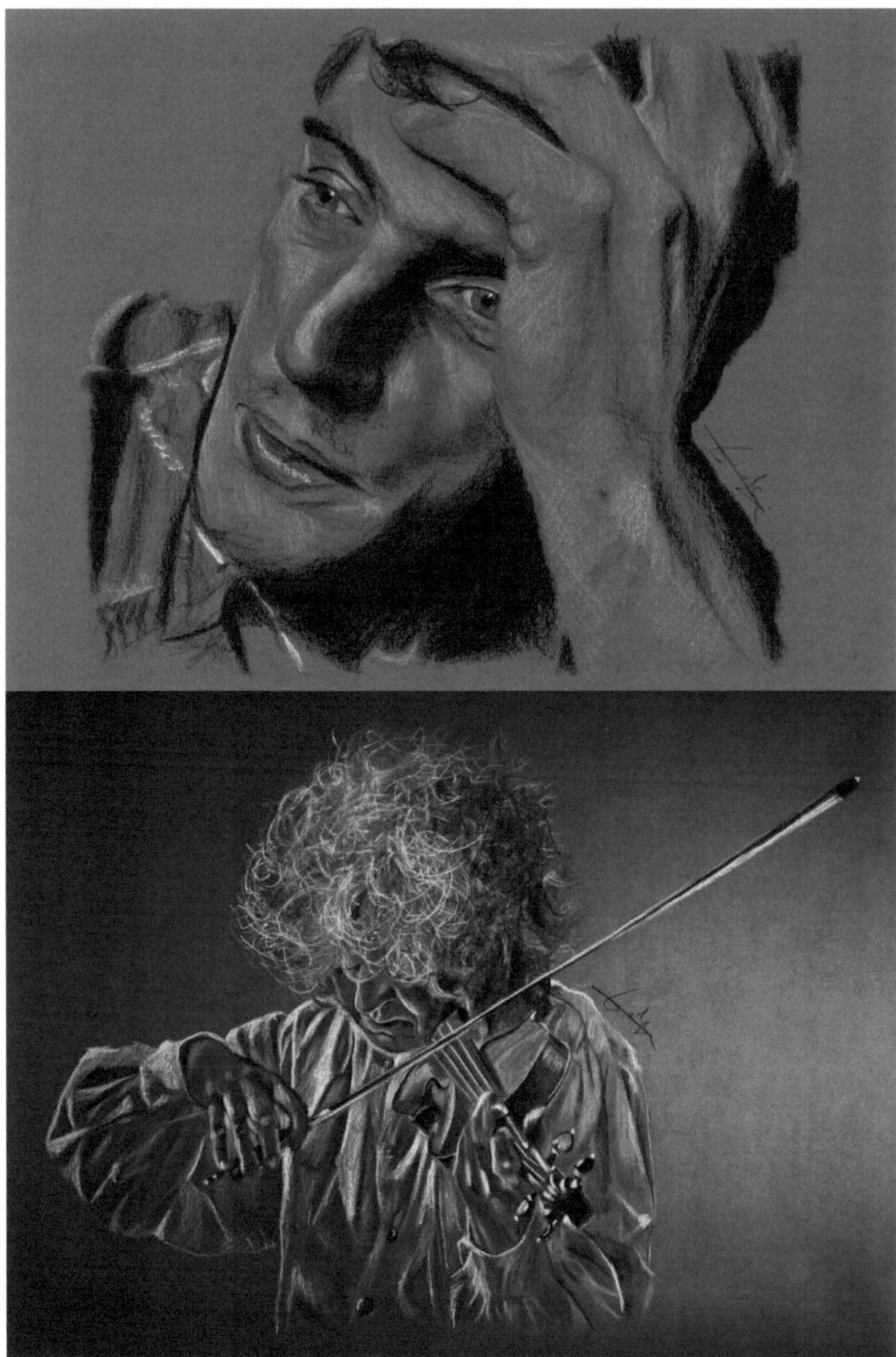

84 Portraits in Chiaroscuro – Philippe Flohic

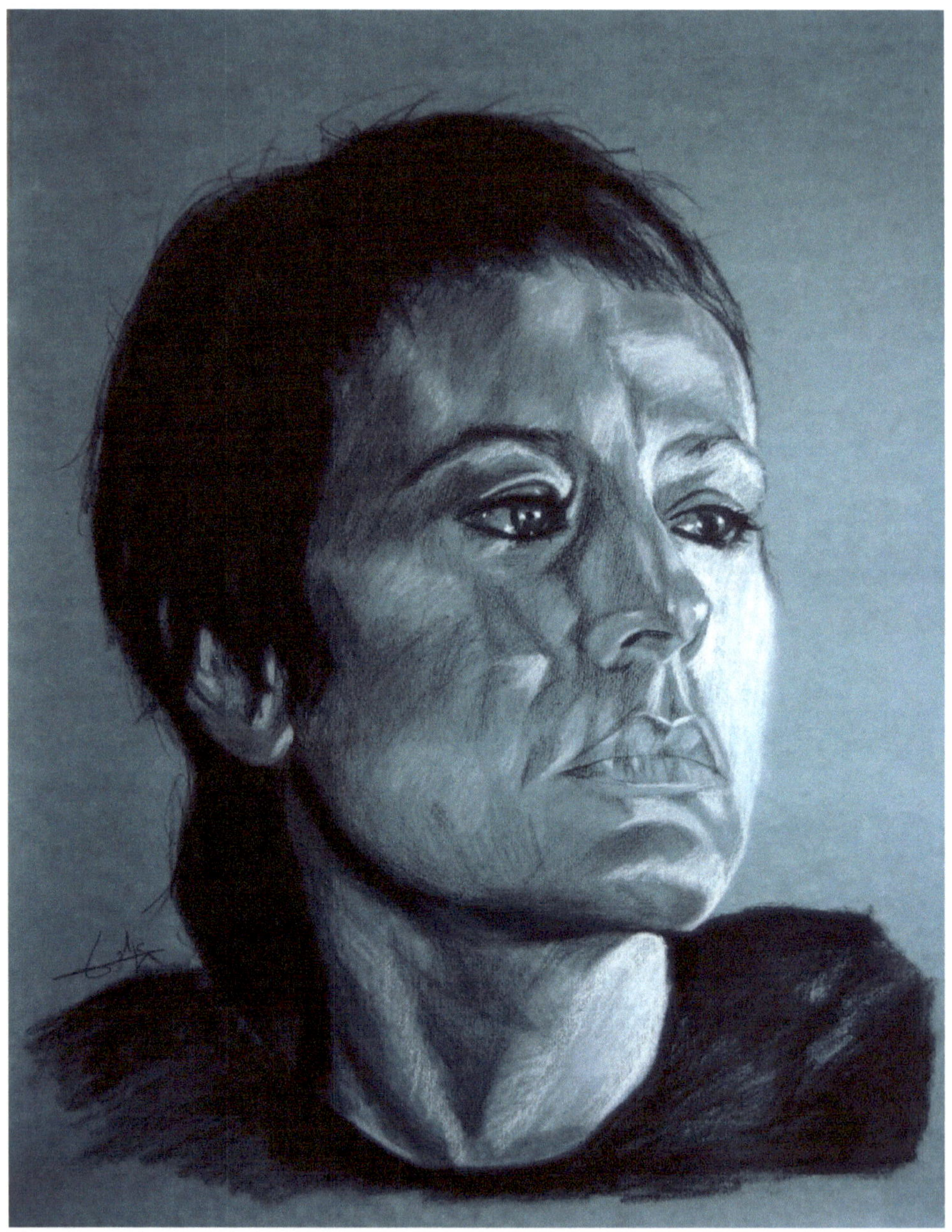

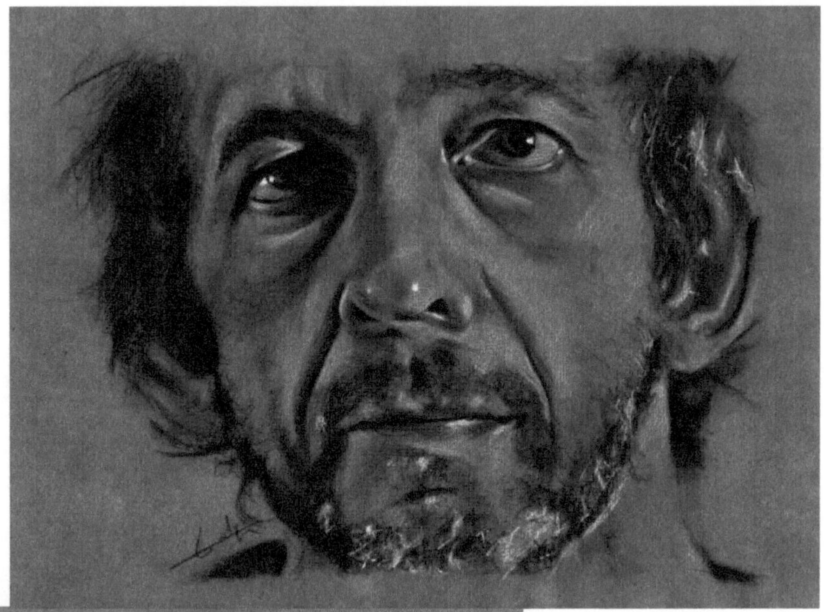

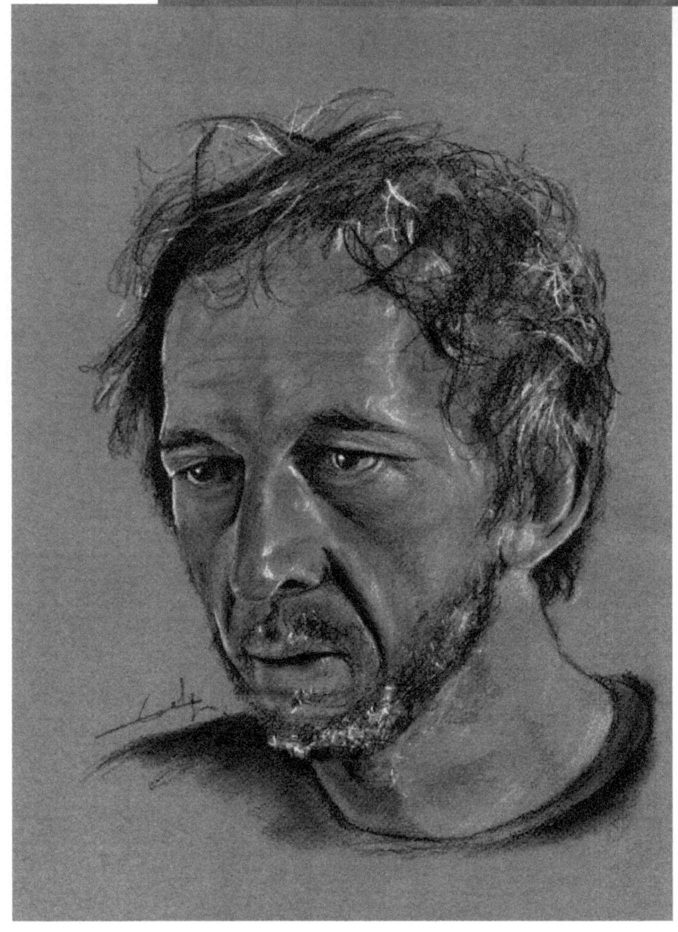

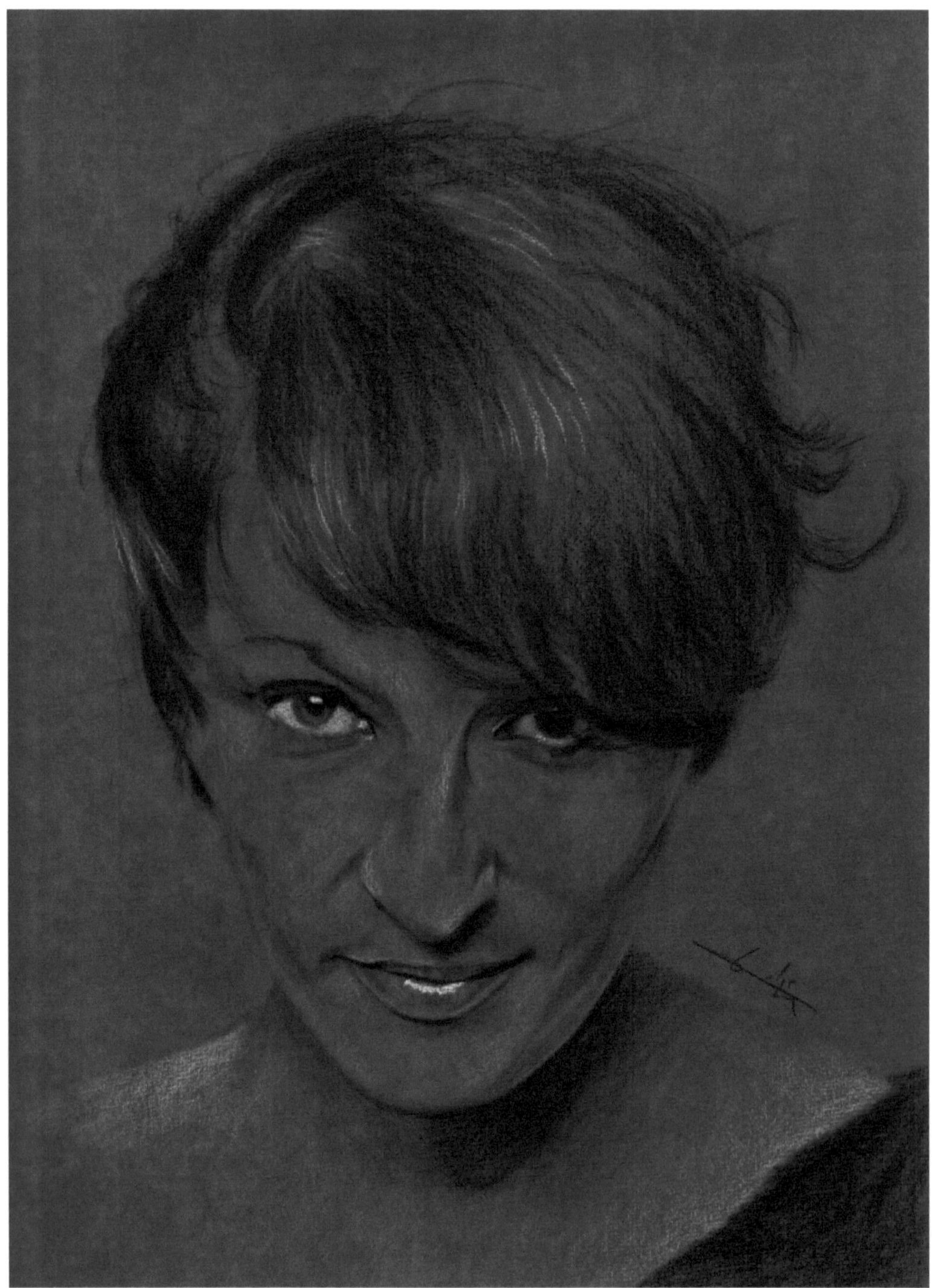

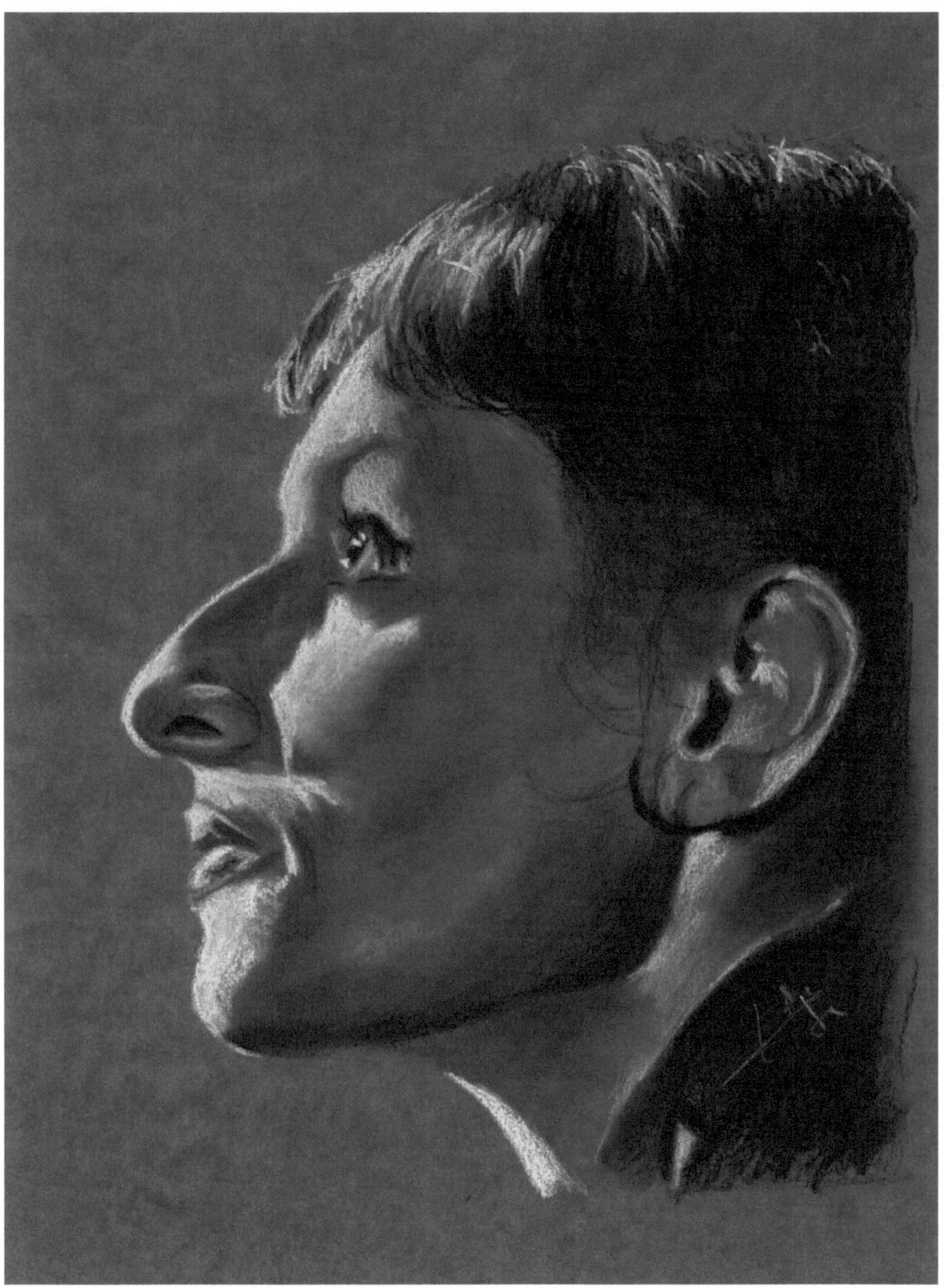

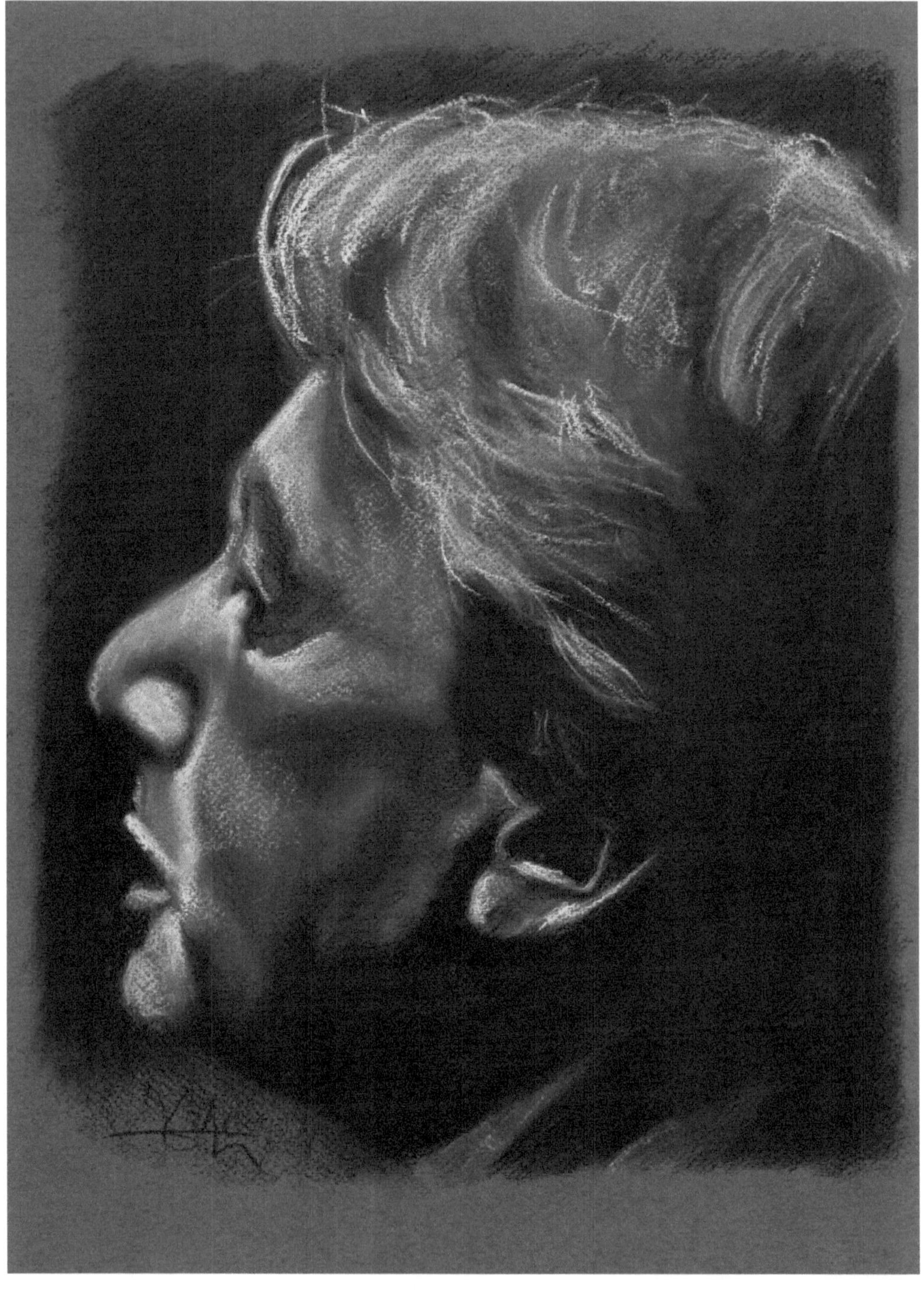

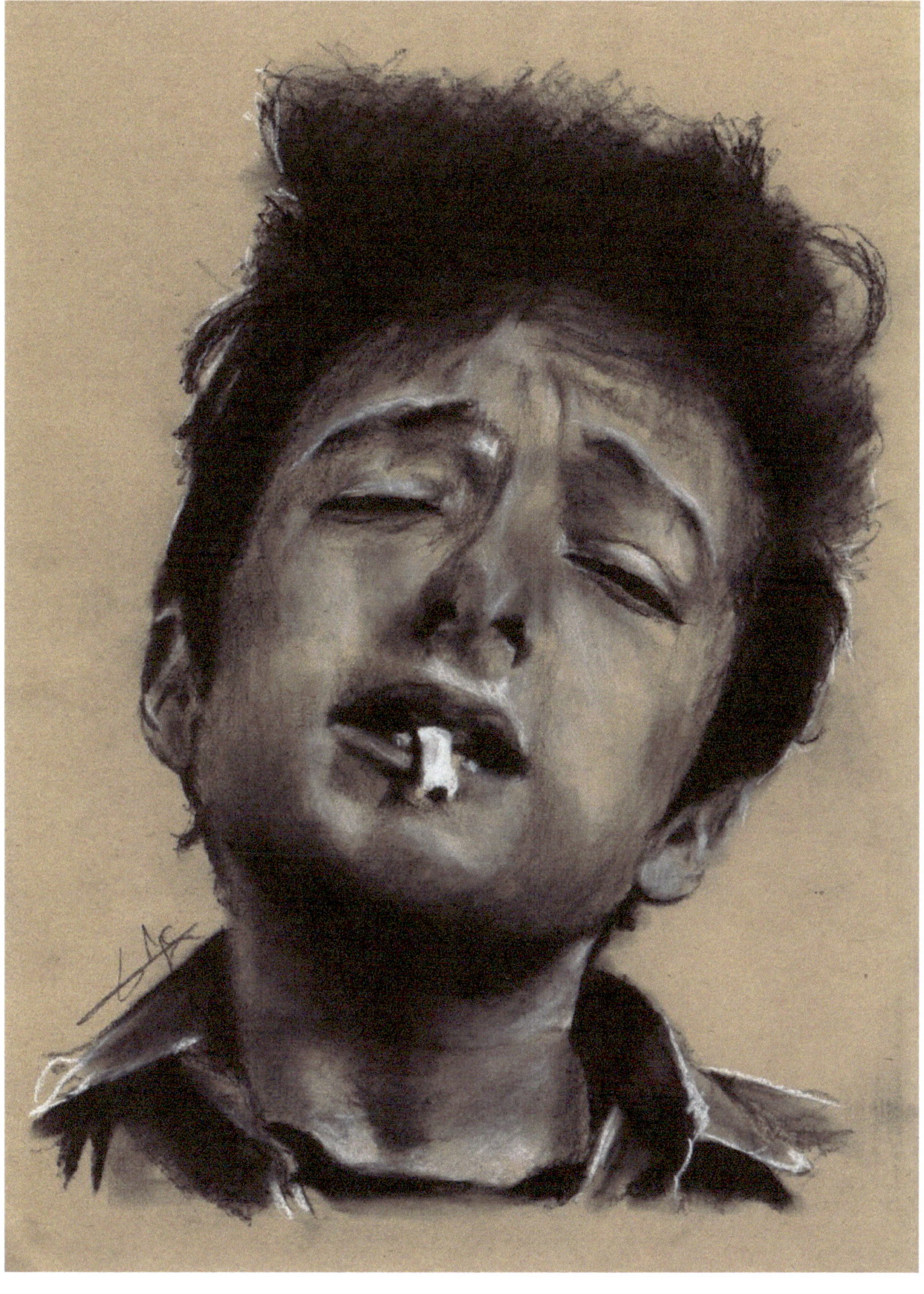

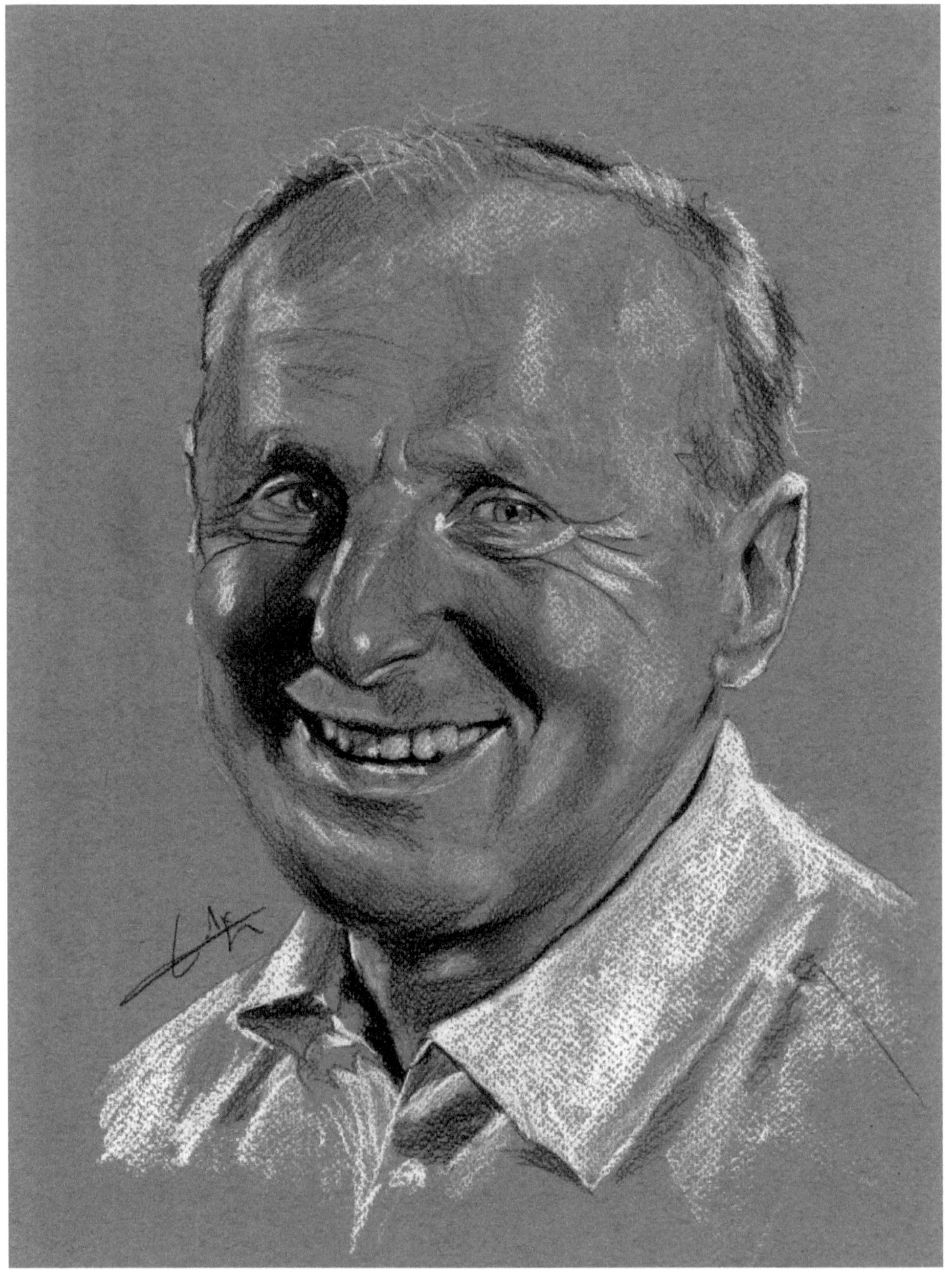

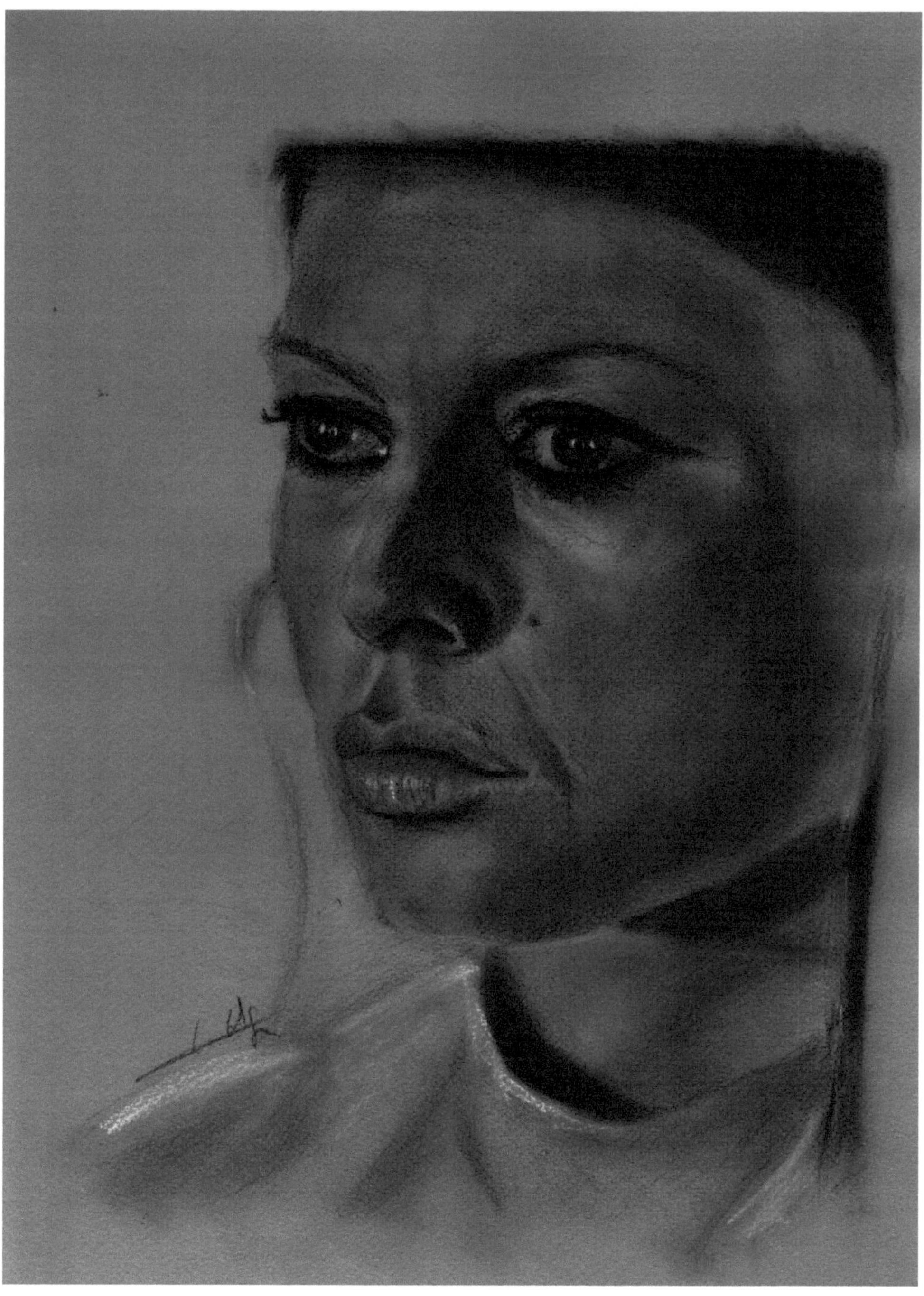

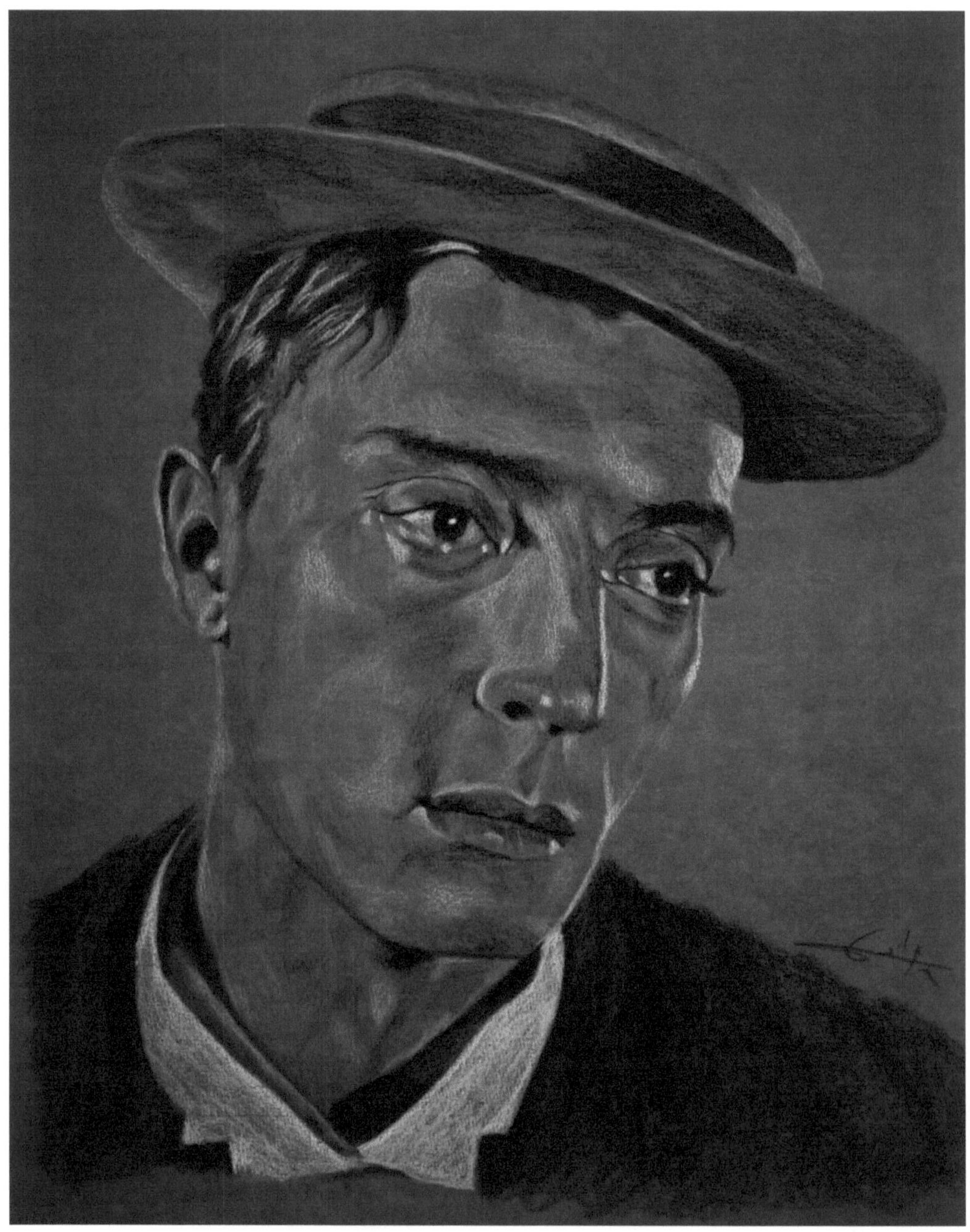

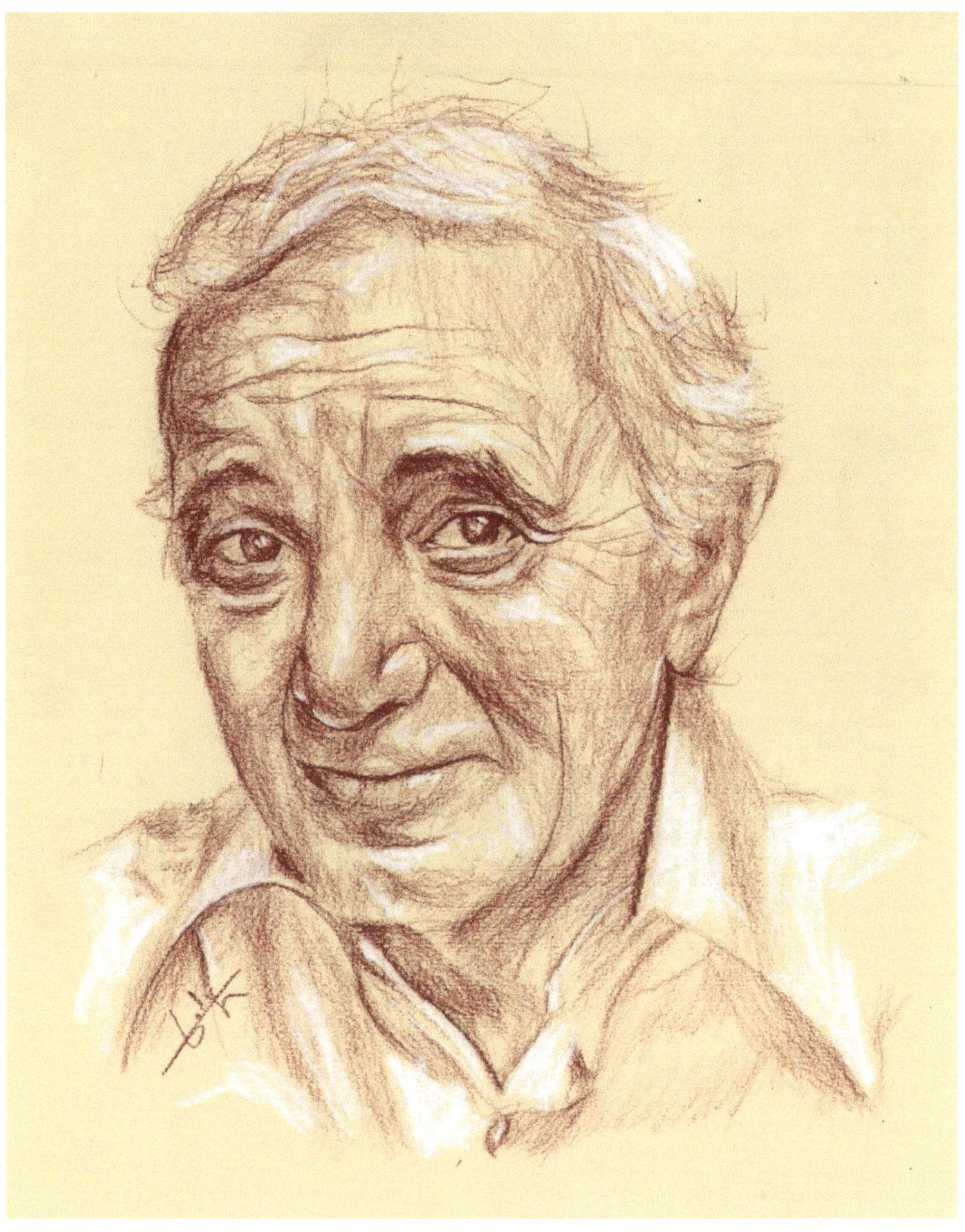

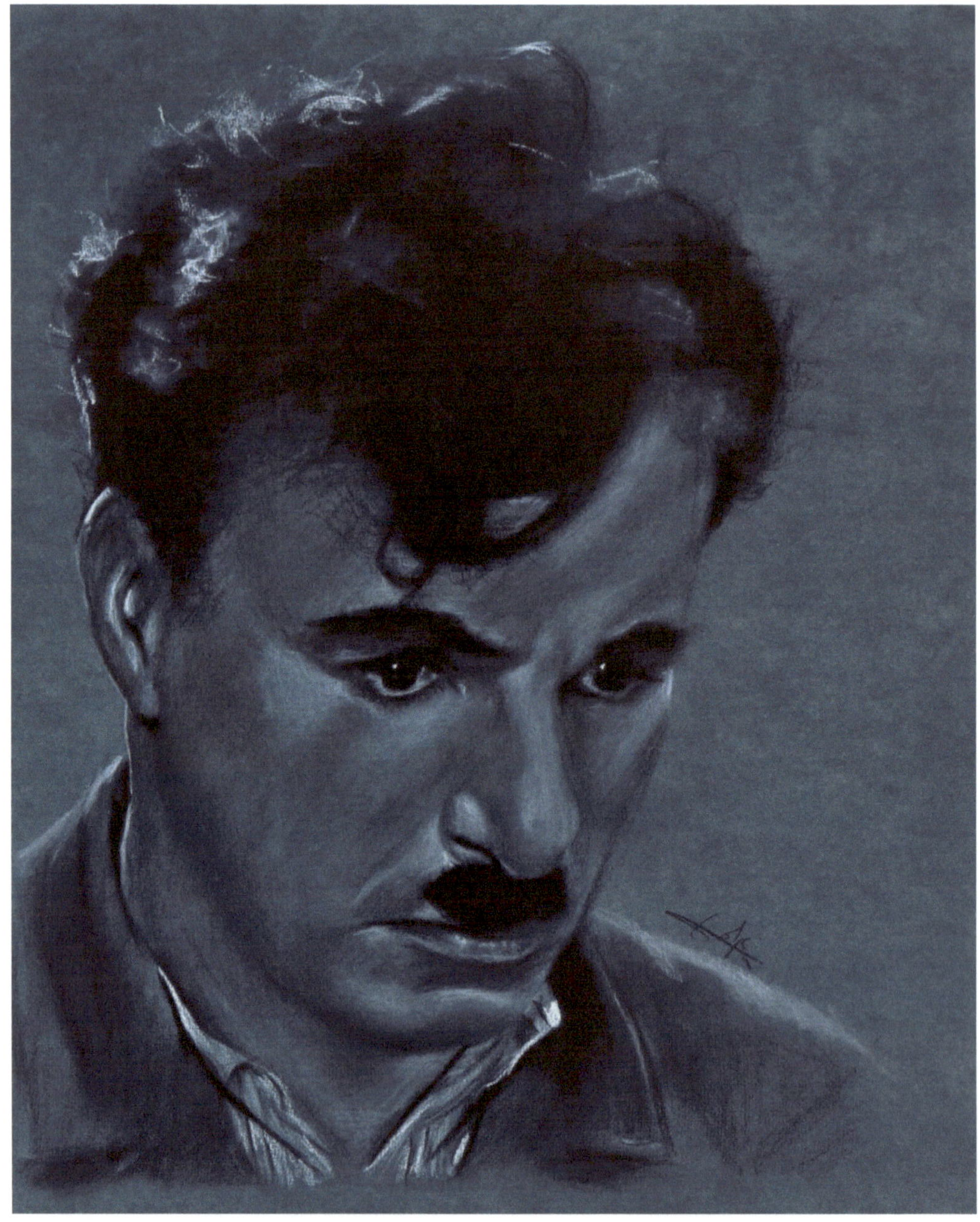

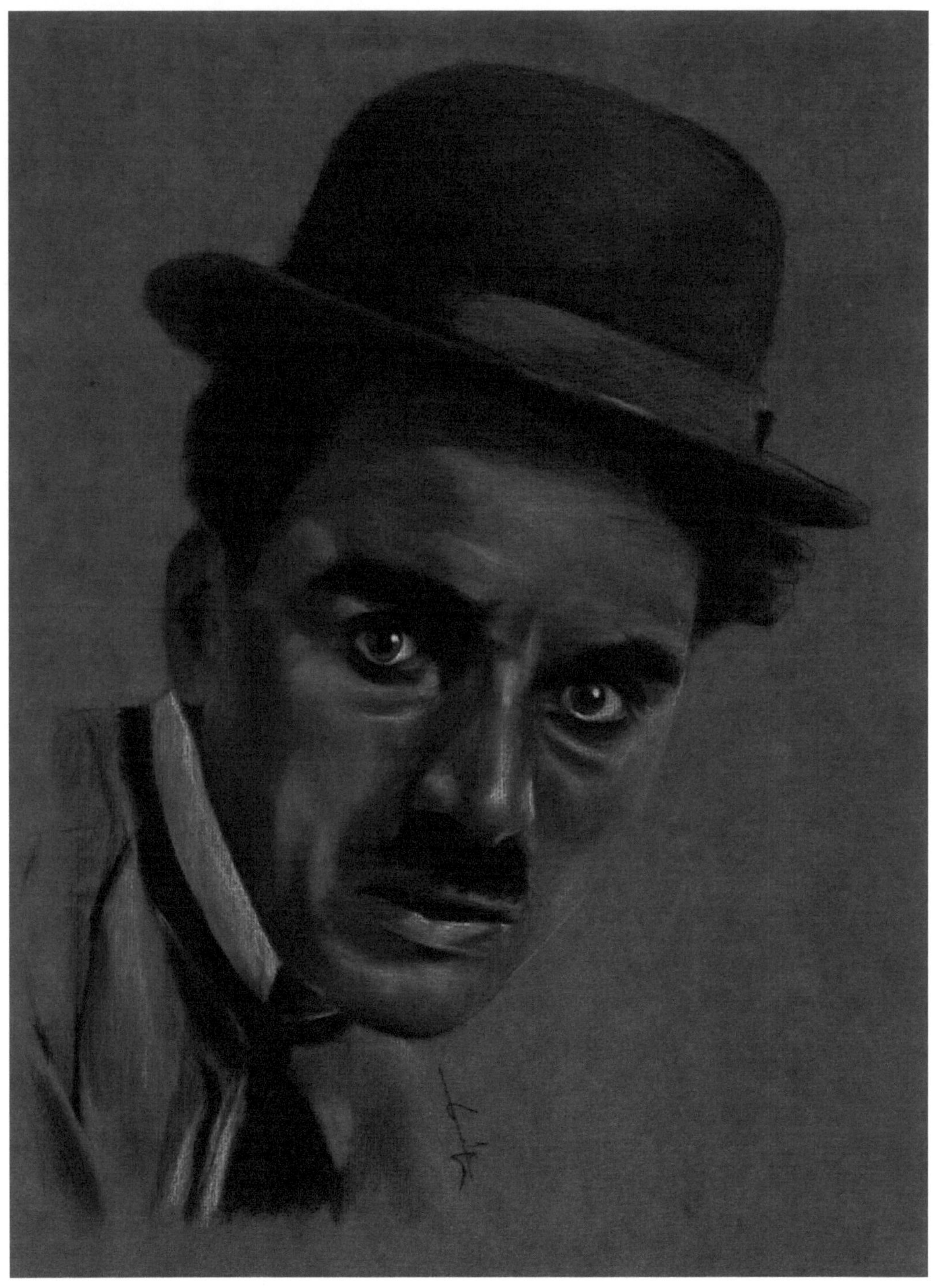

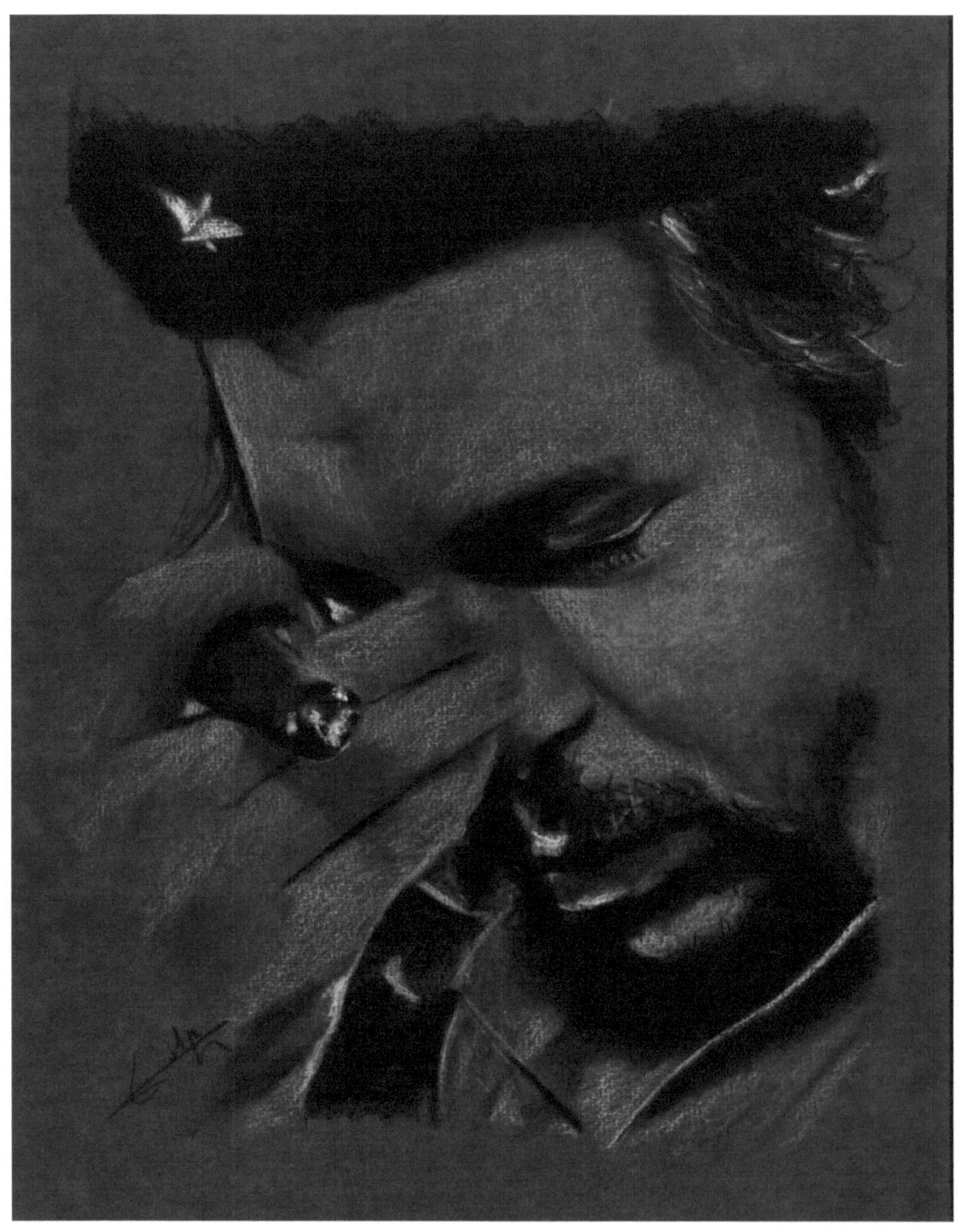

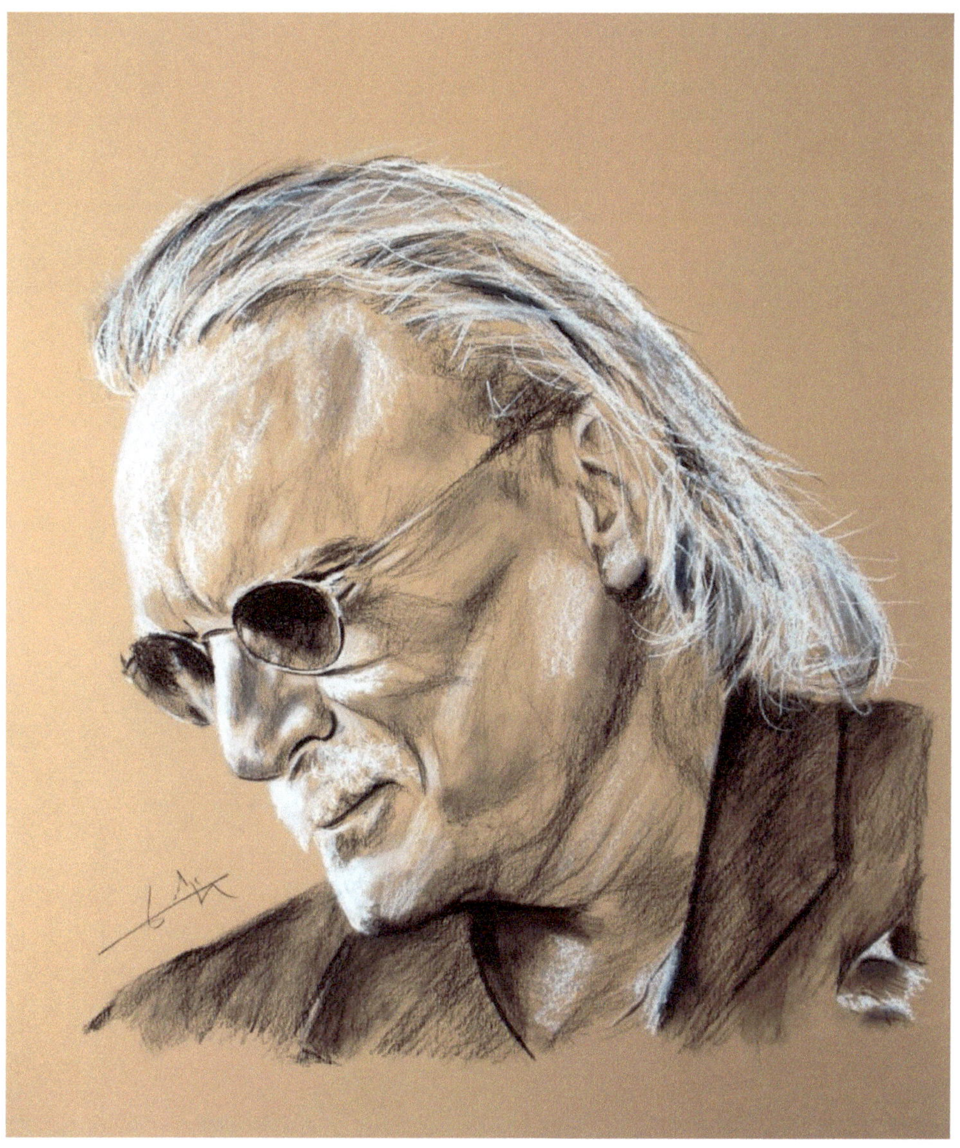

18

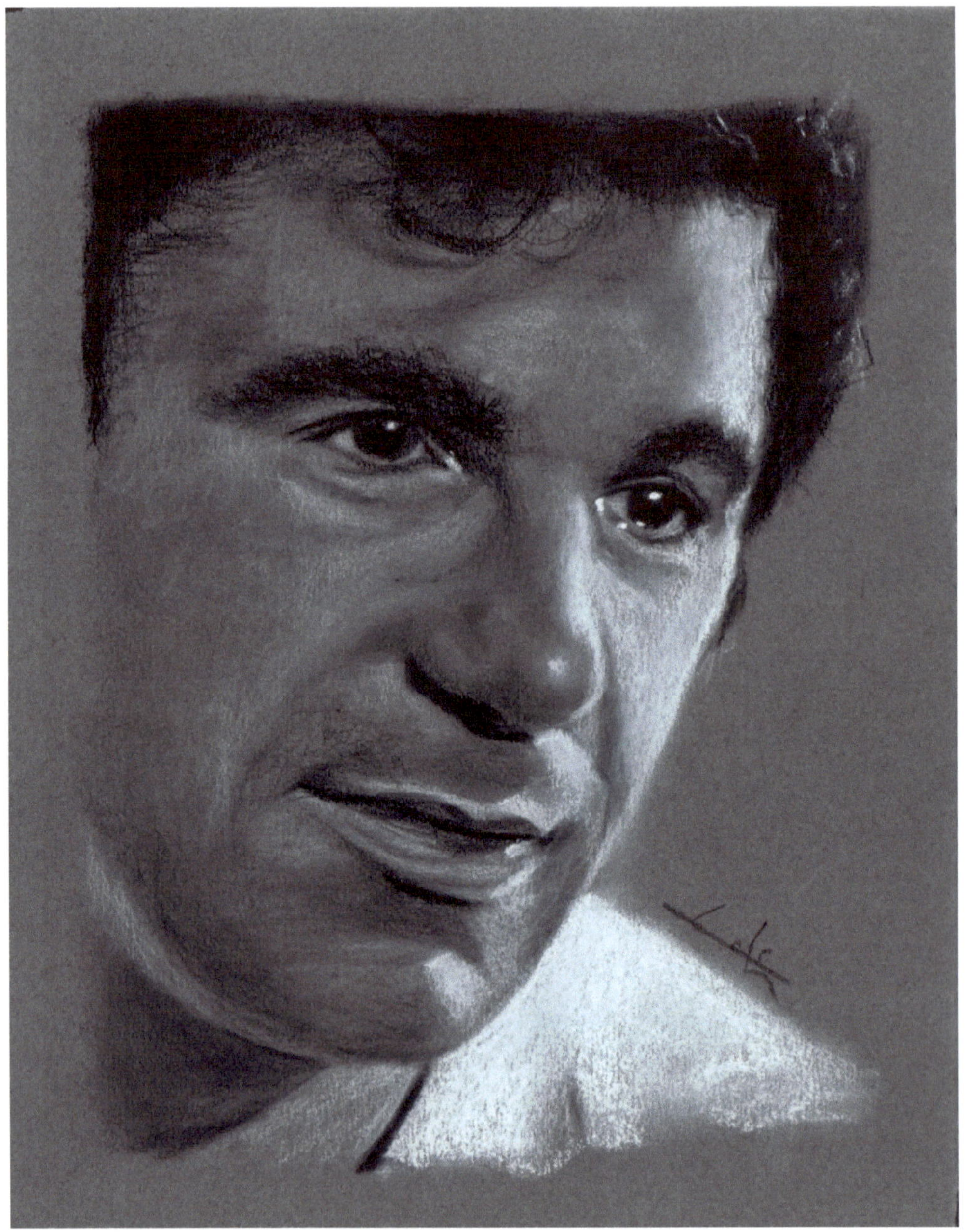

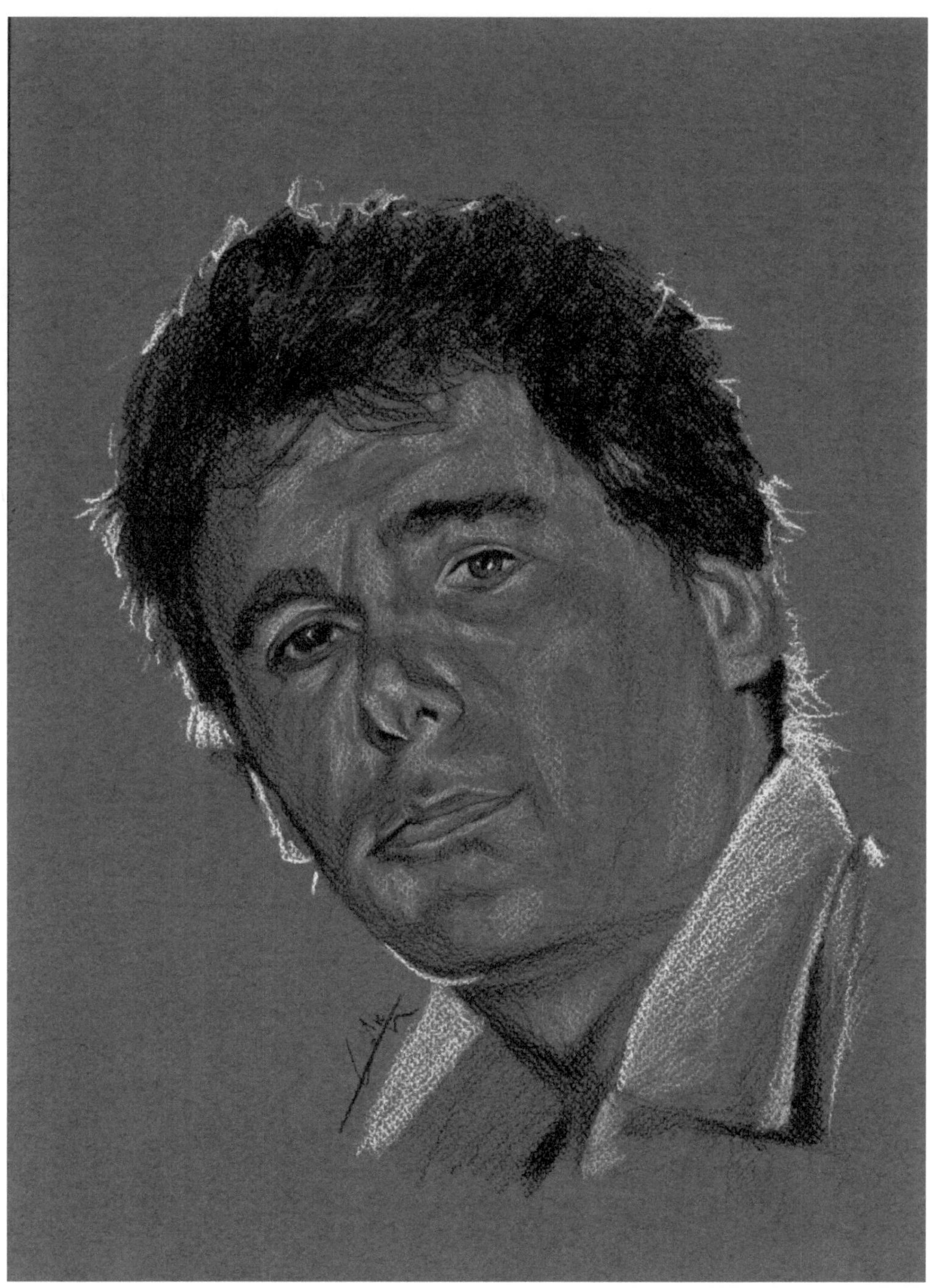

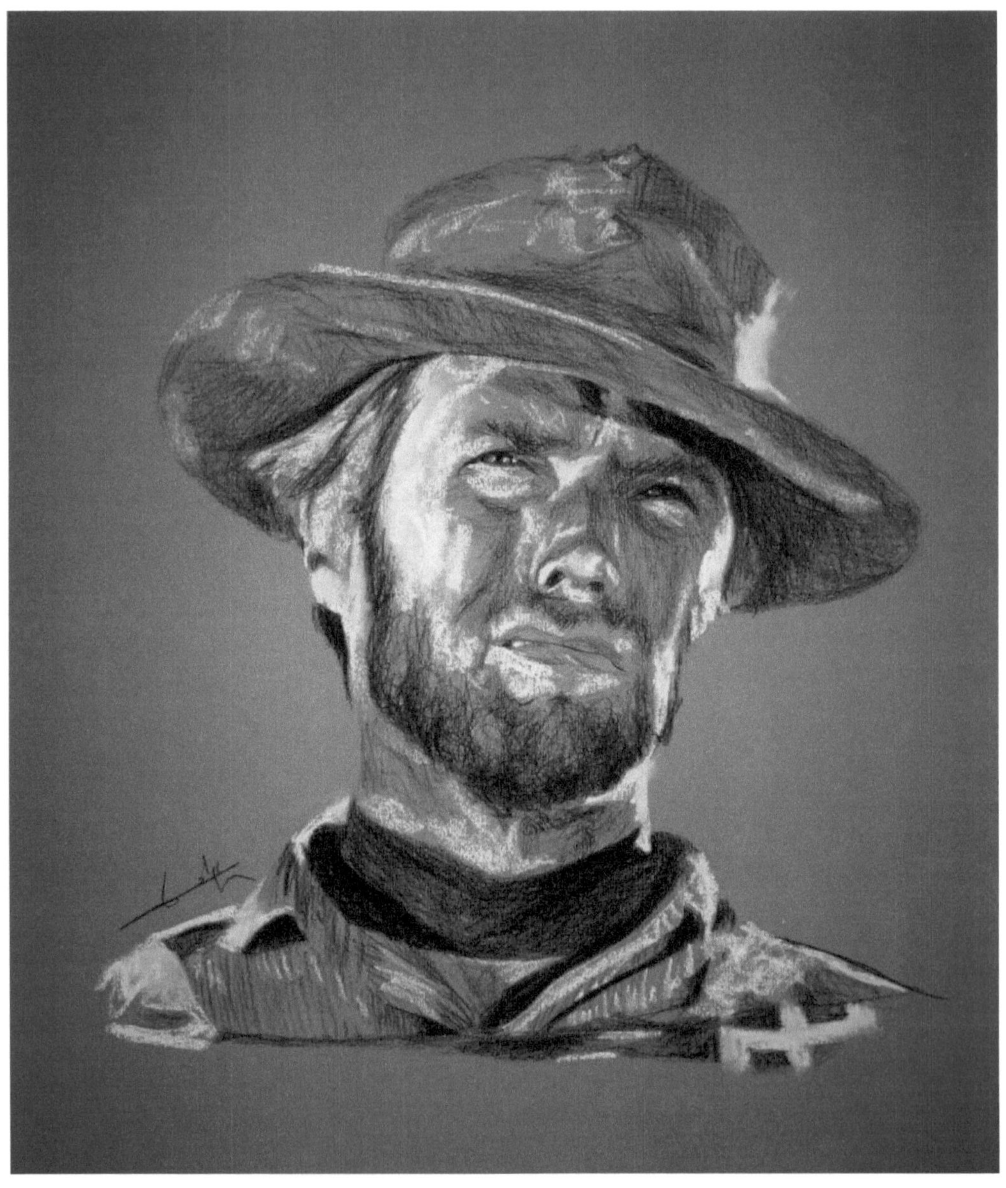

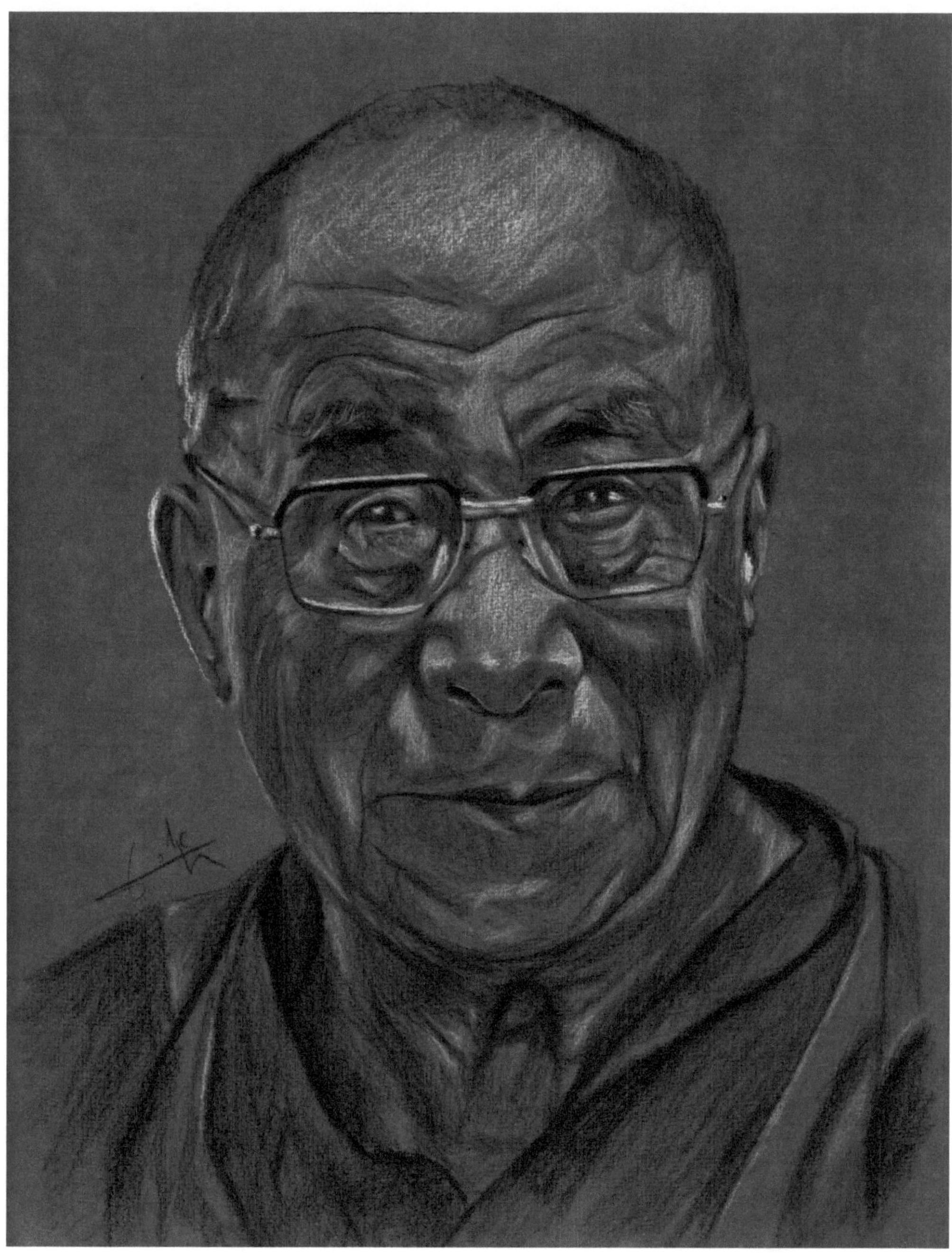

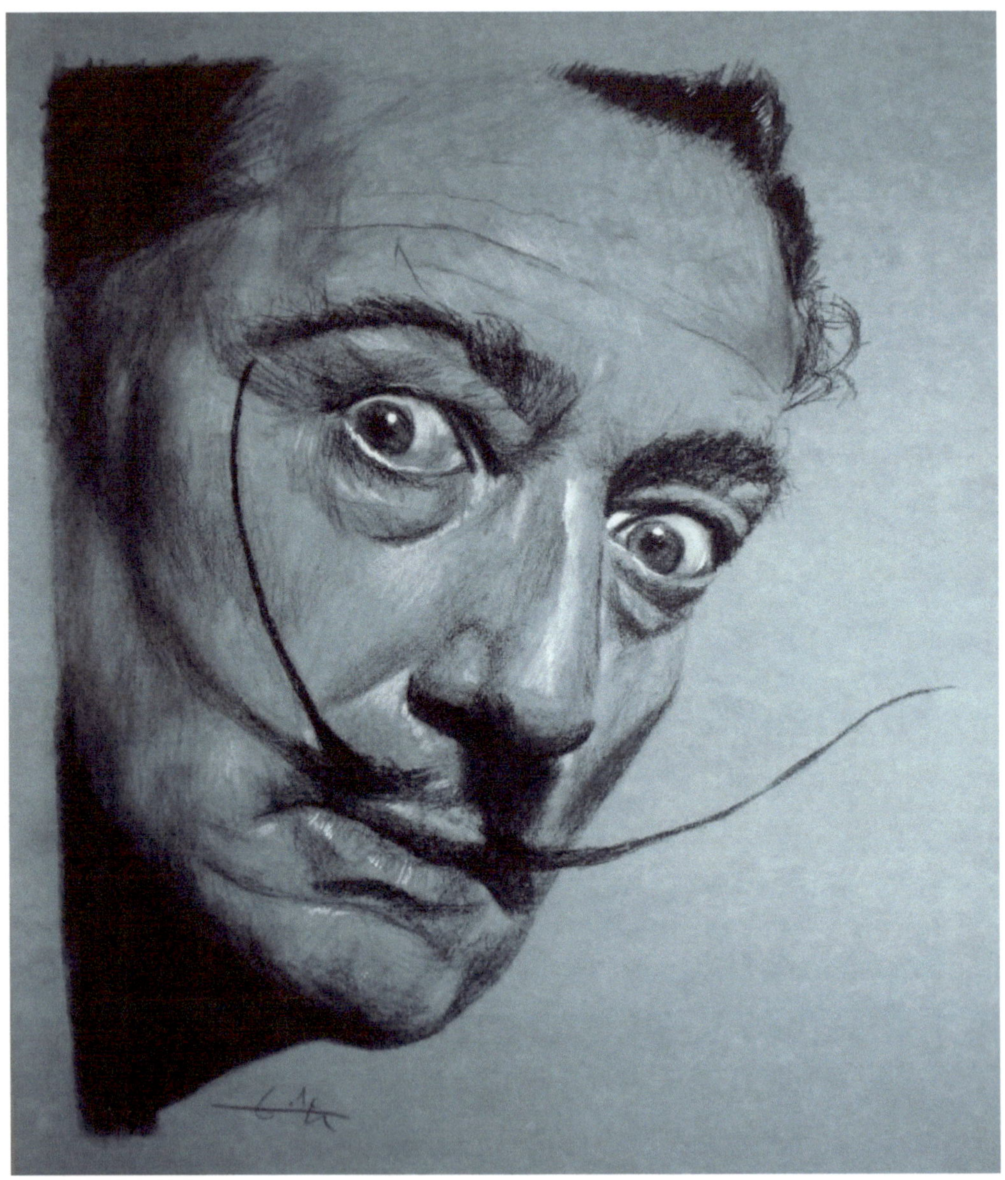

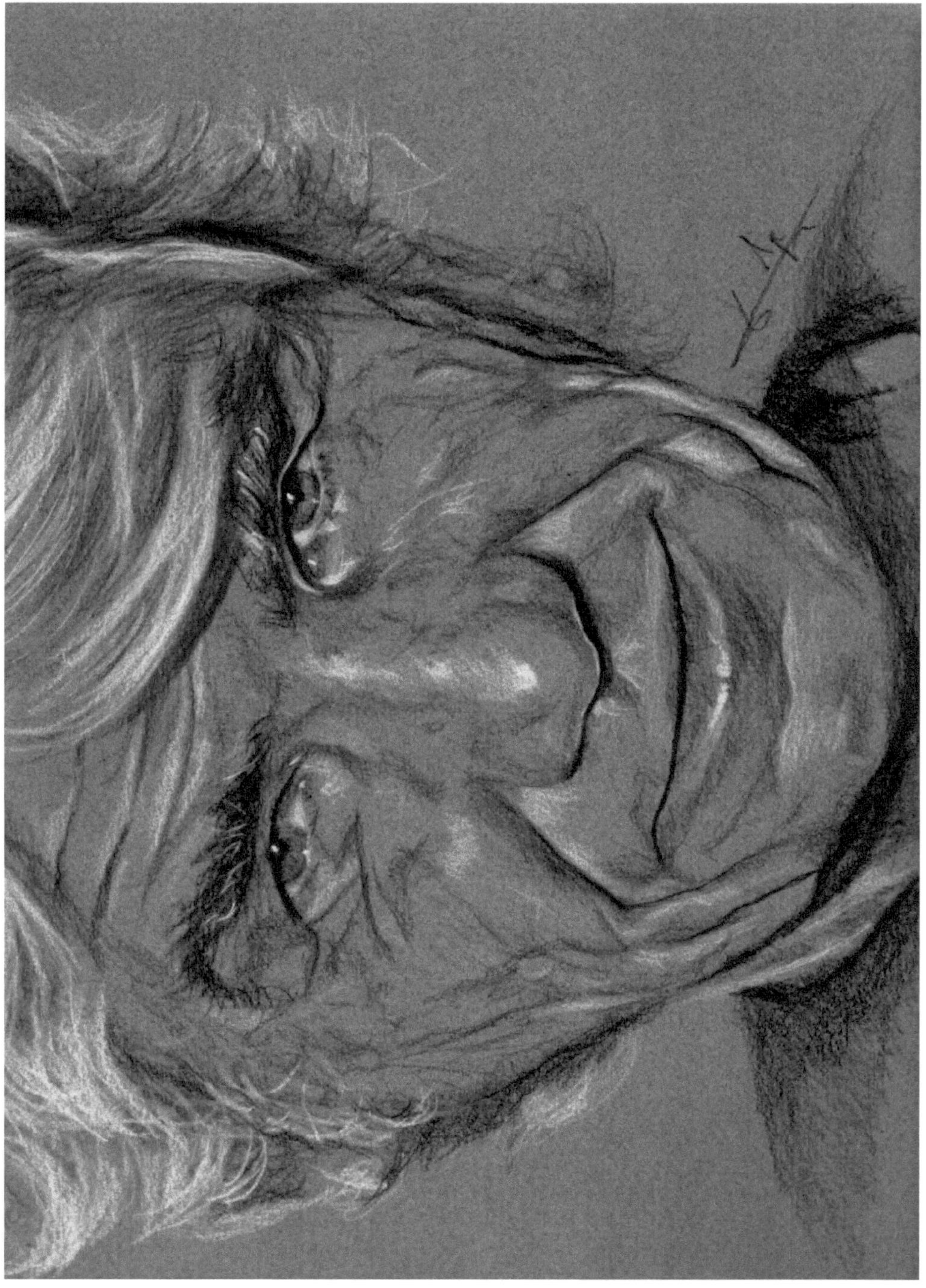

24

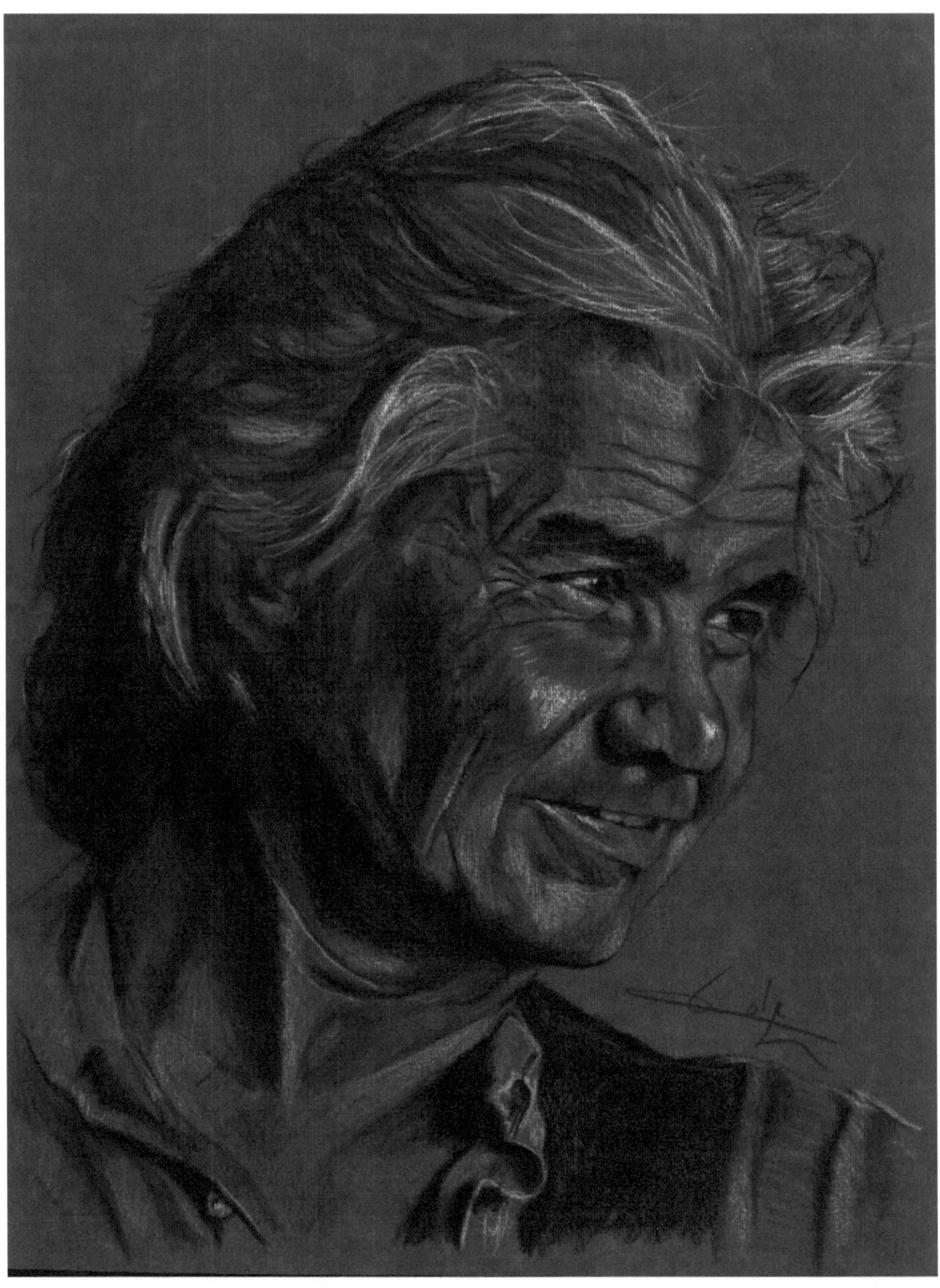

25

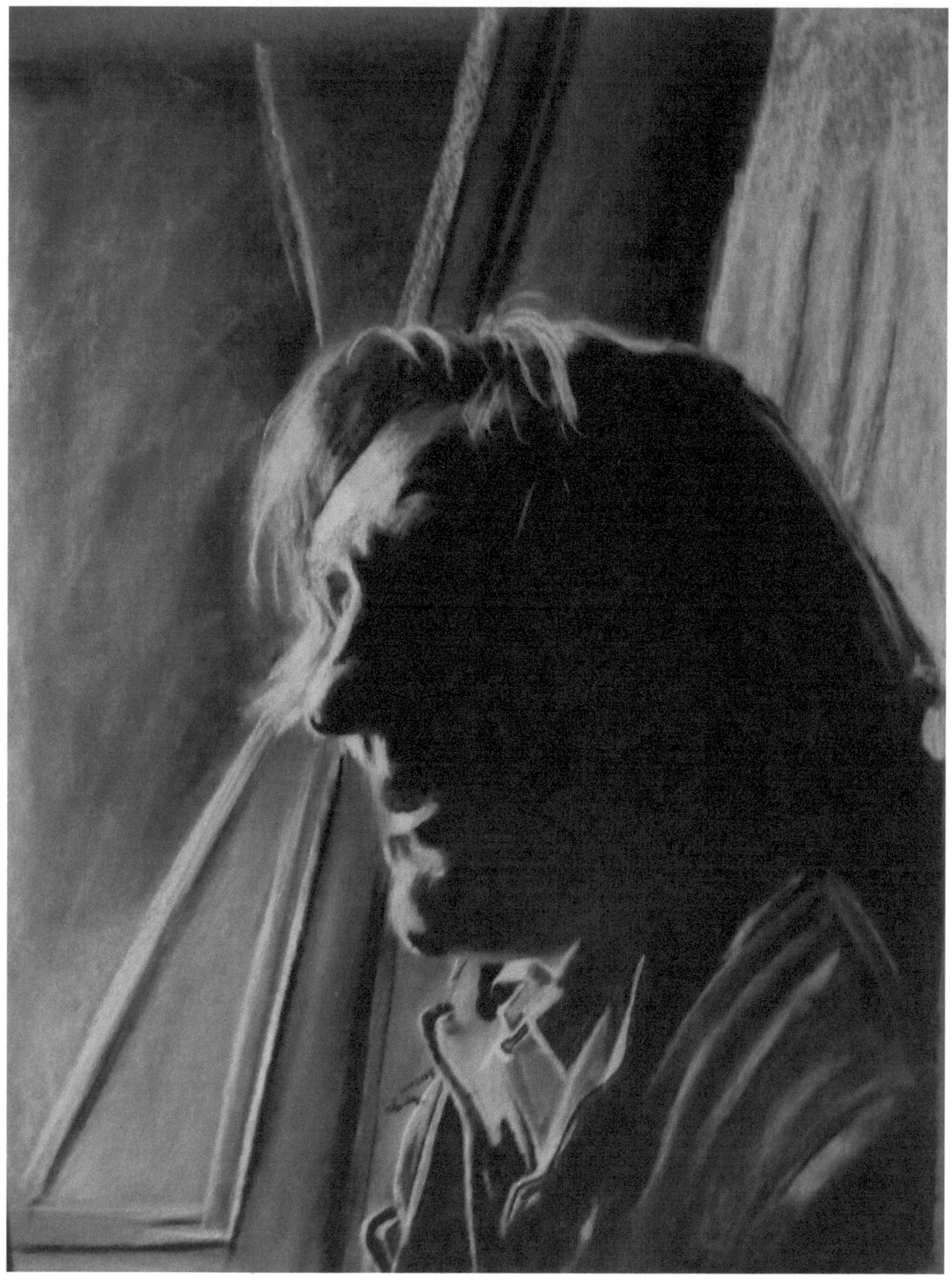

26

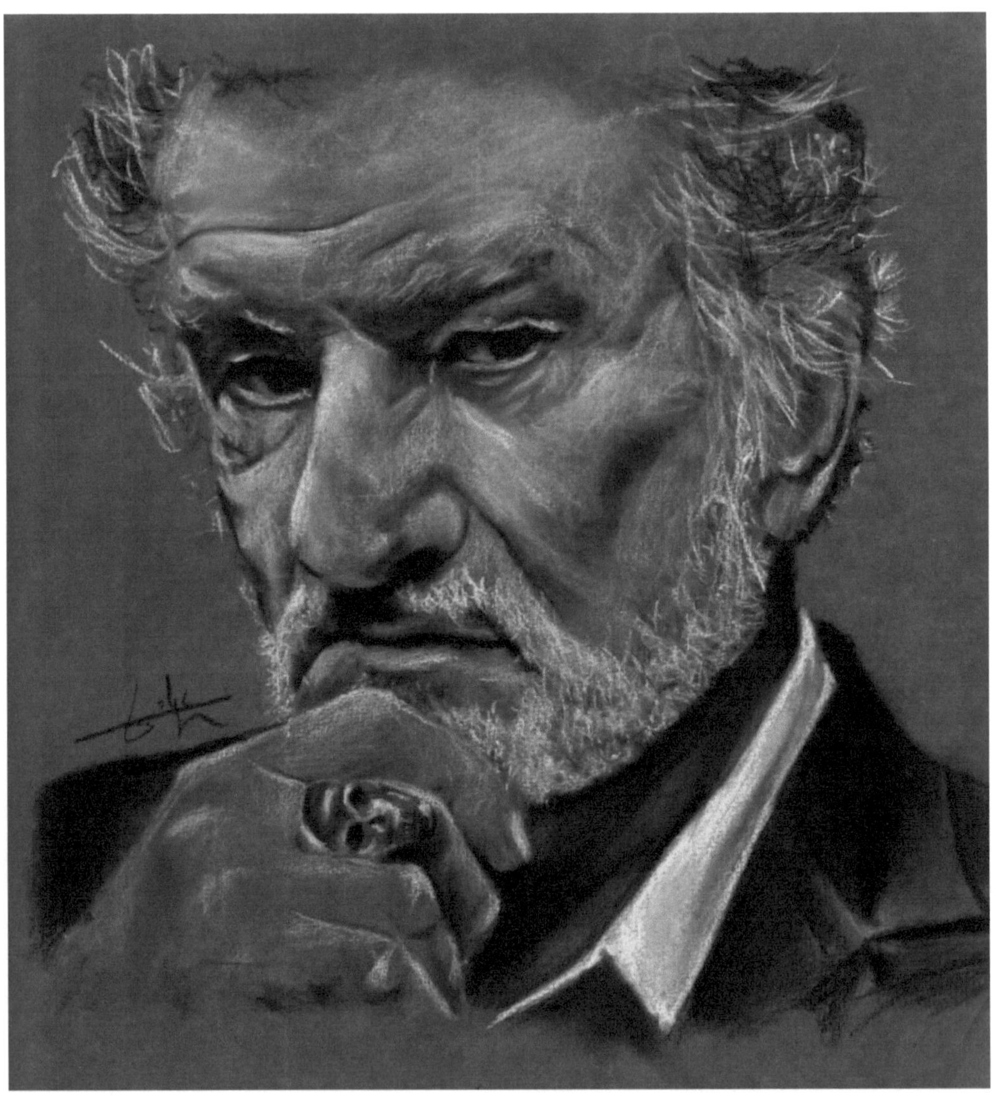

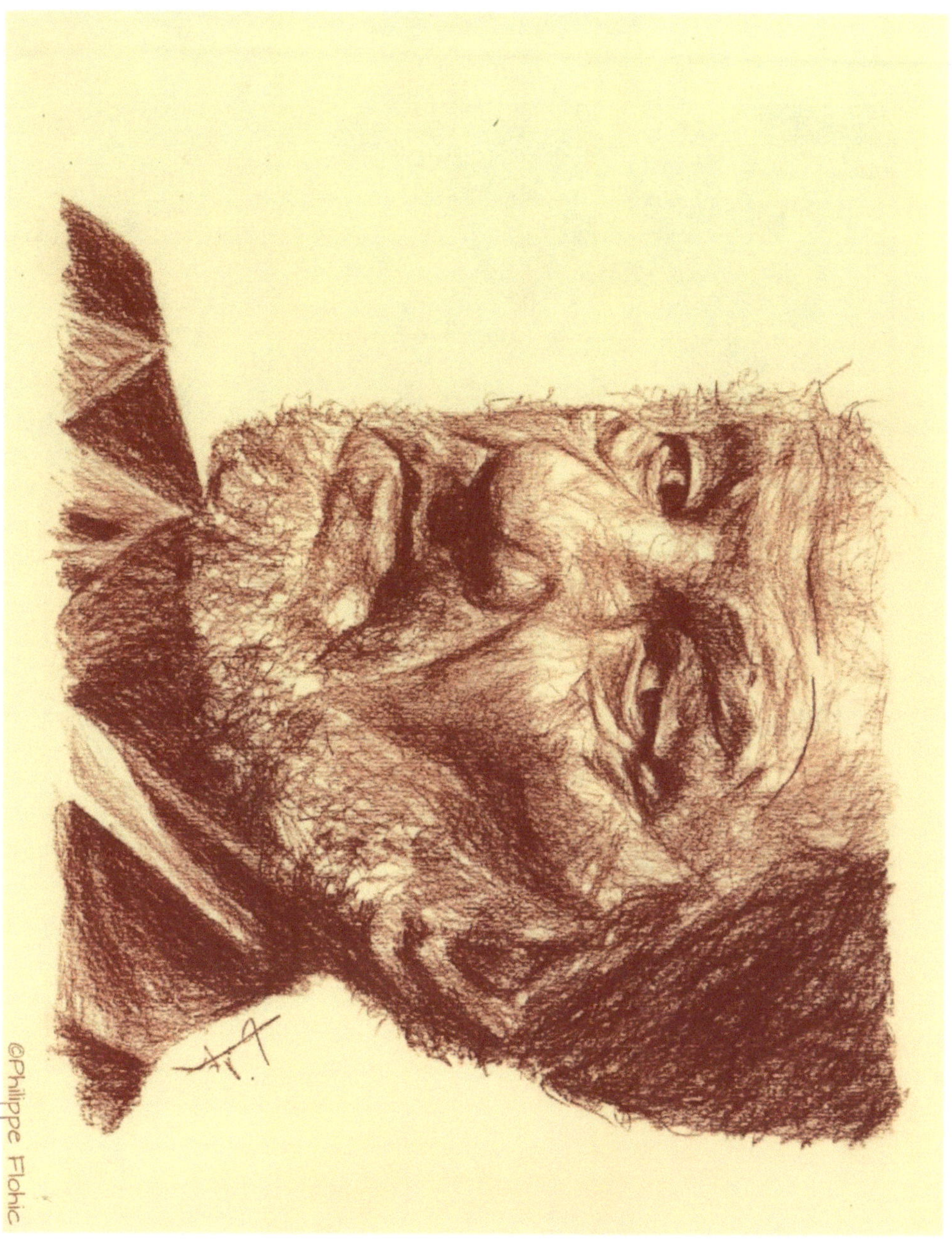
©Philippe Flohic

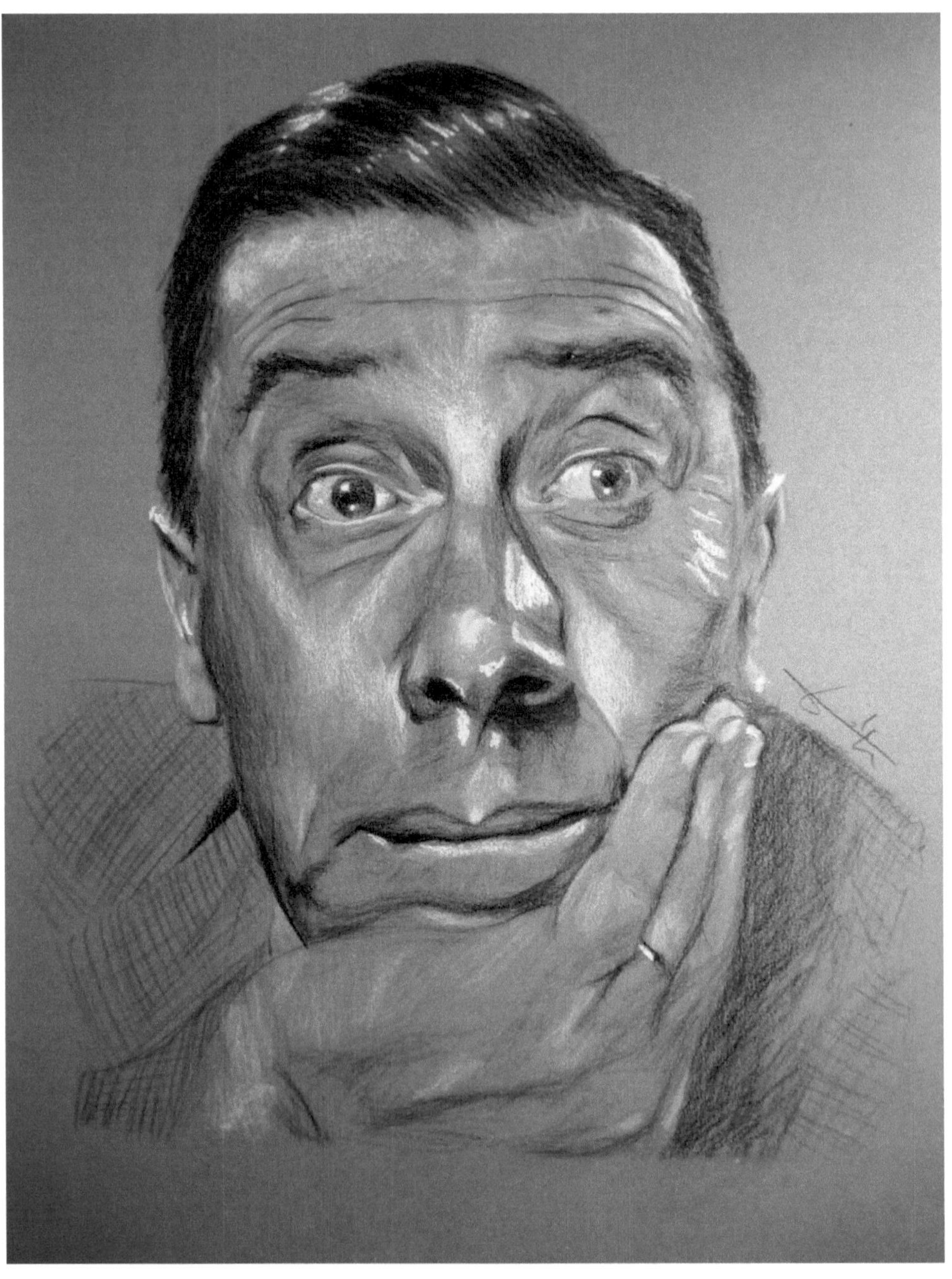

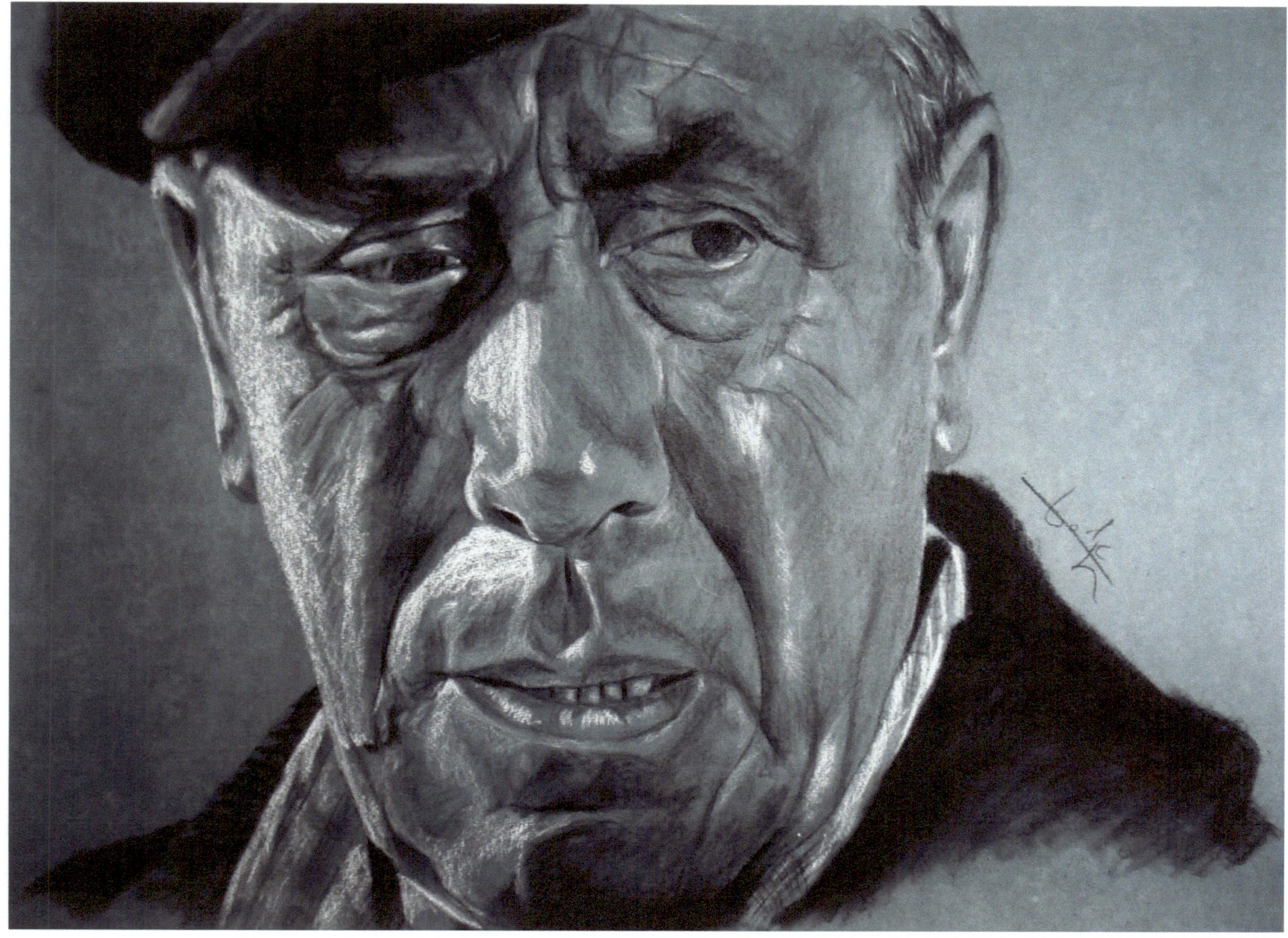

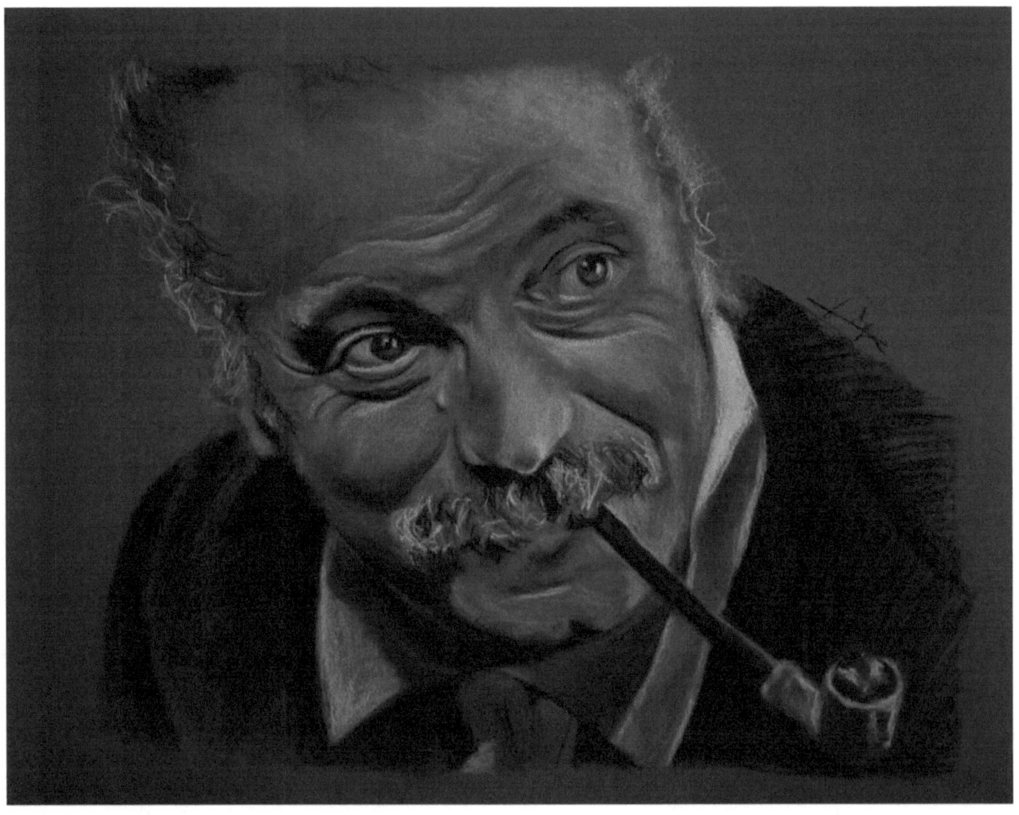

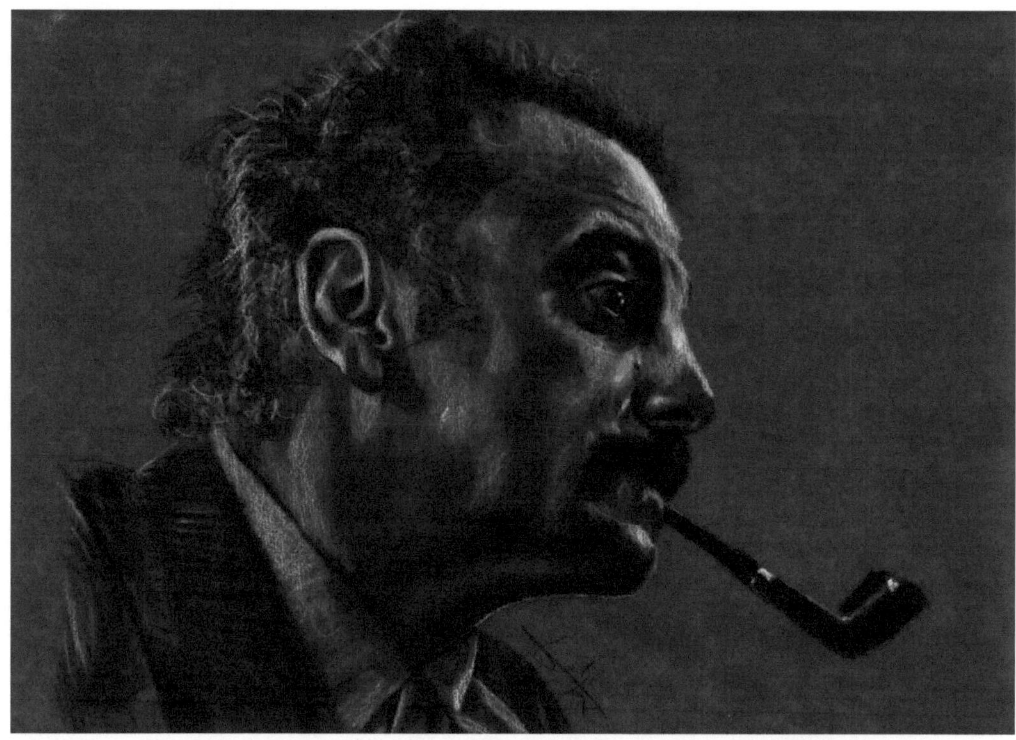

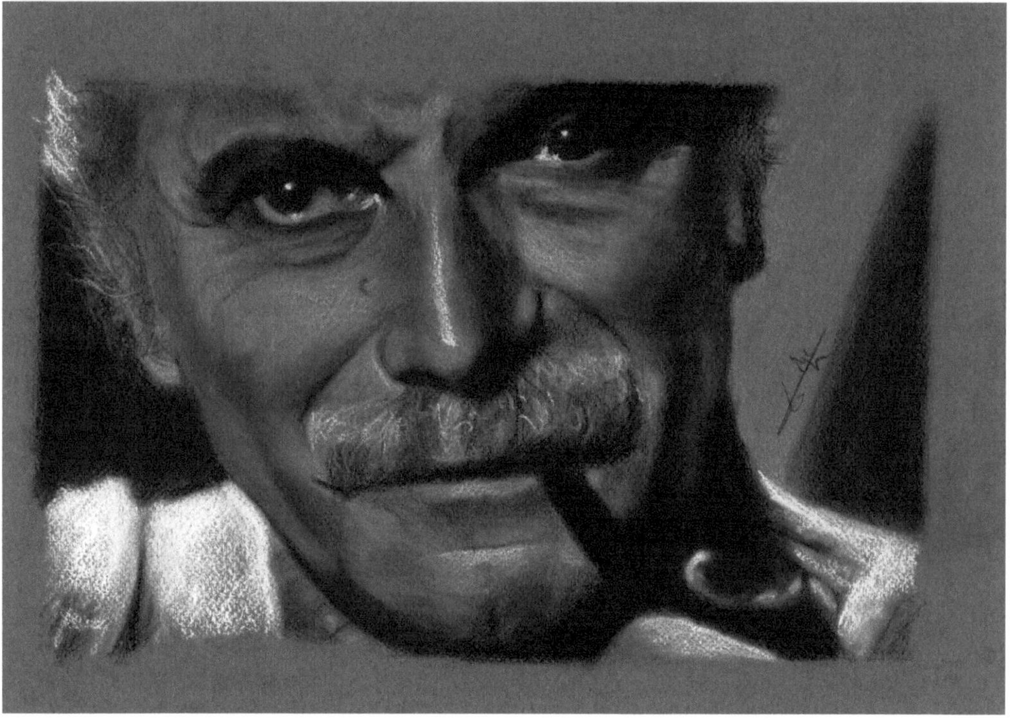

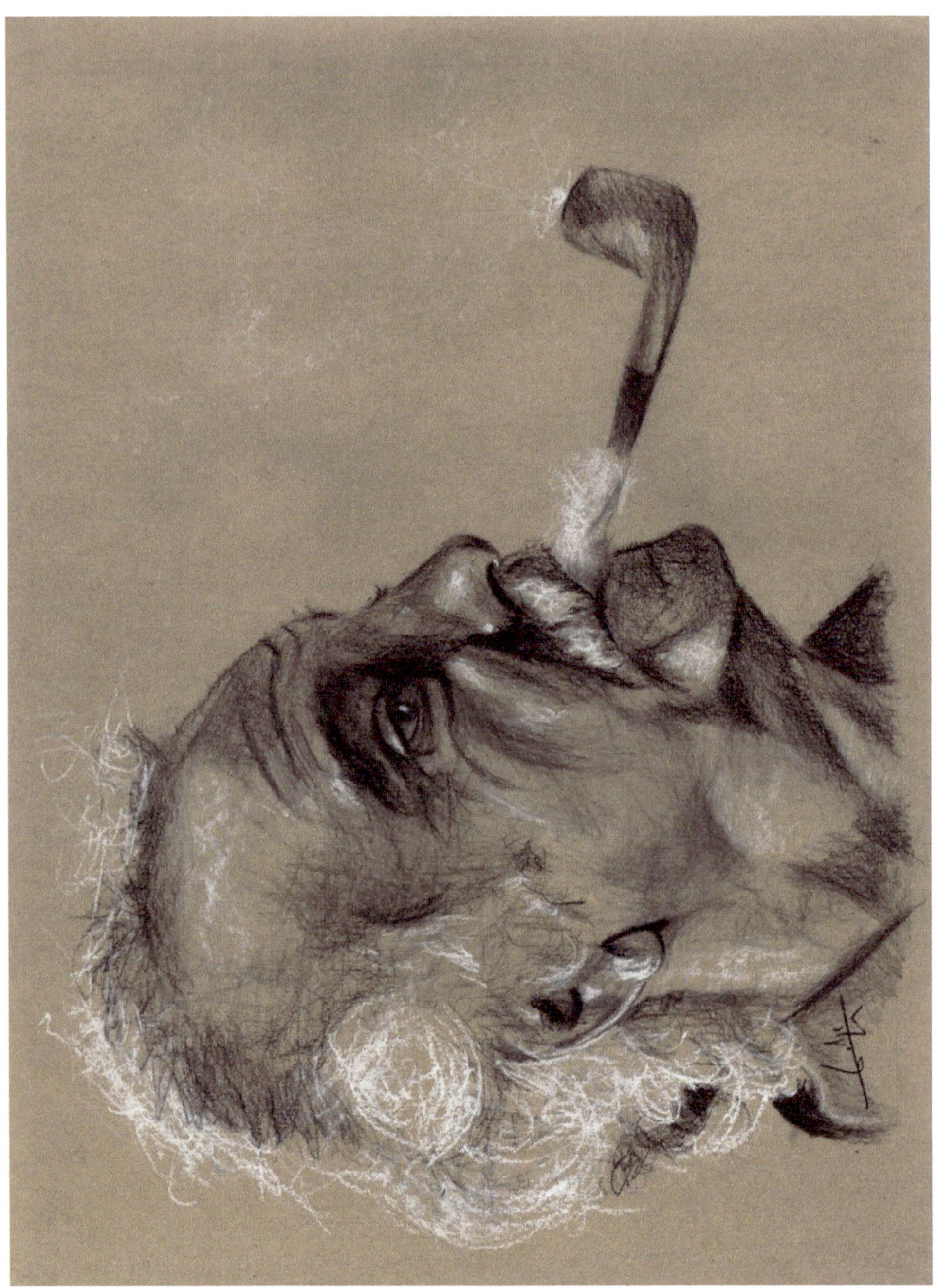

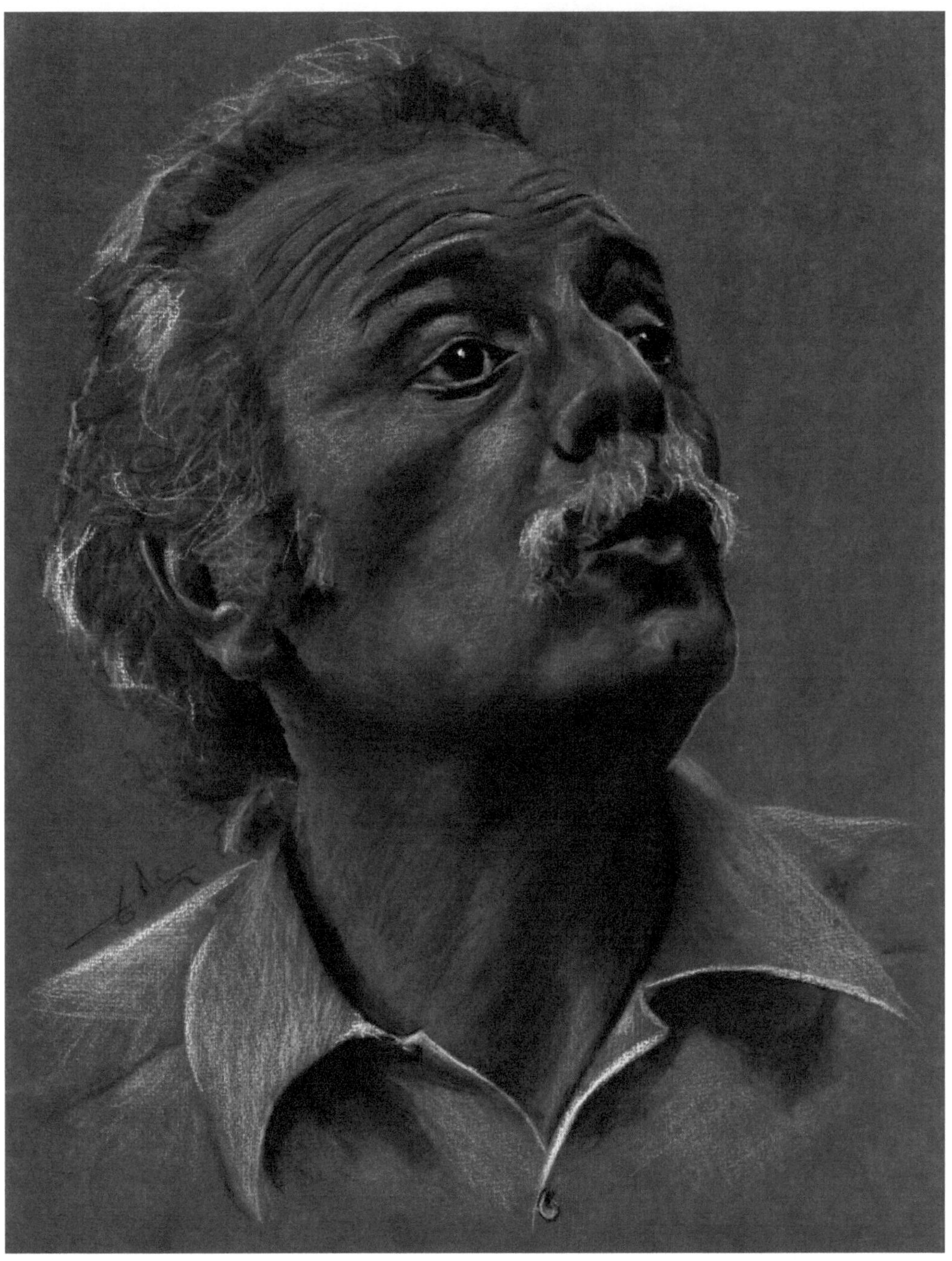

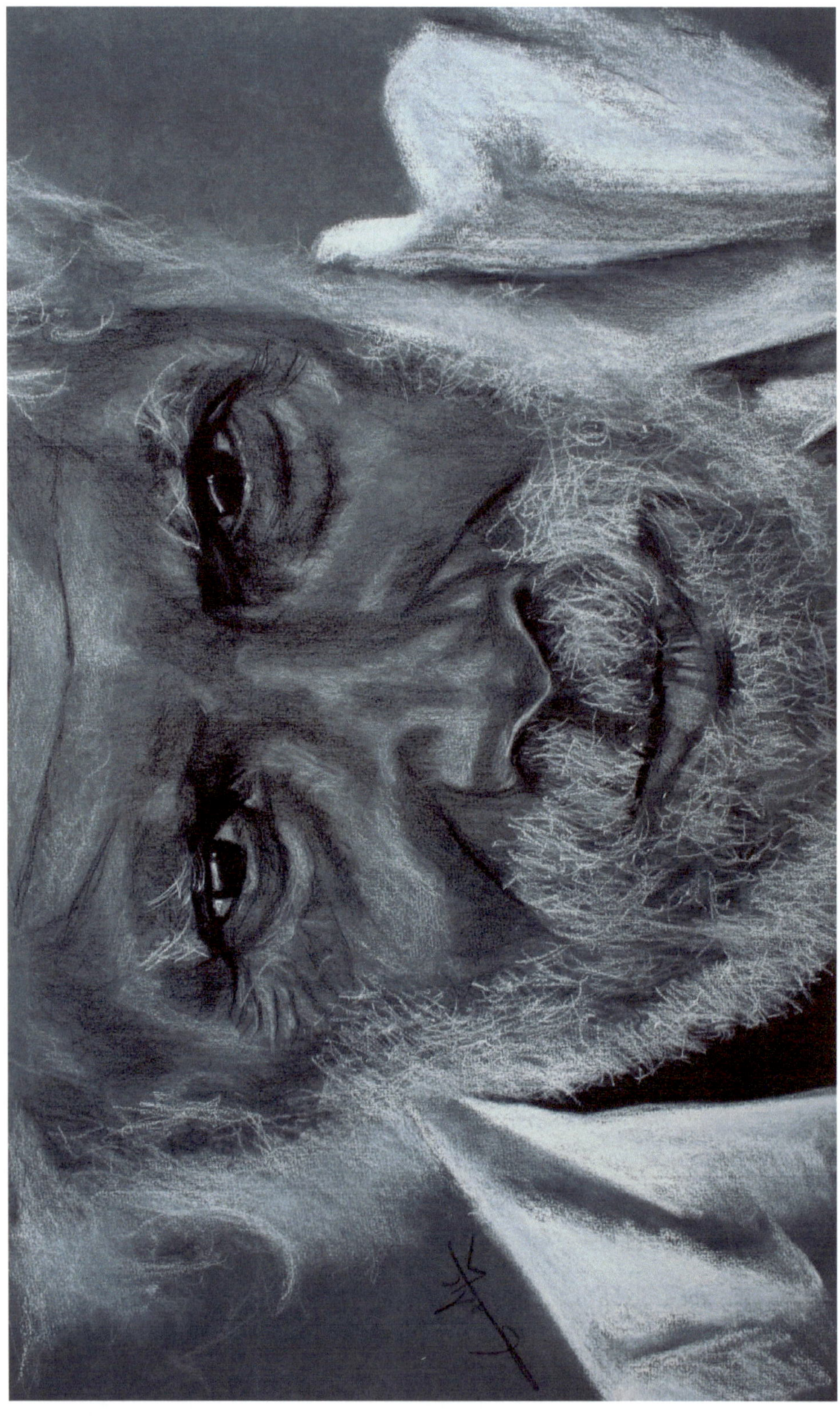

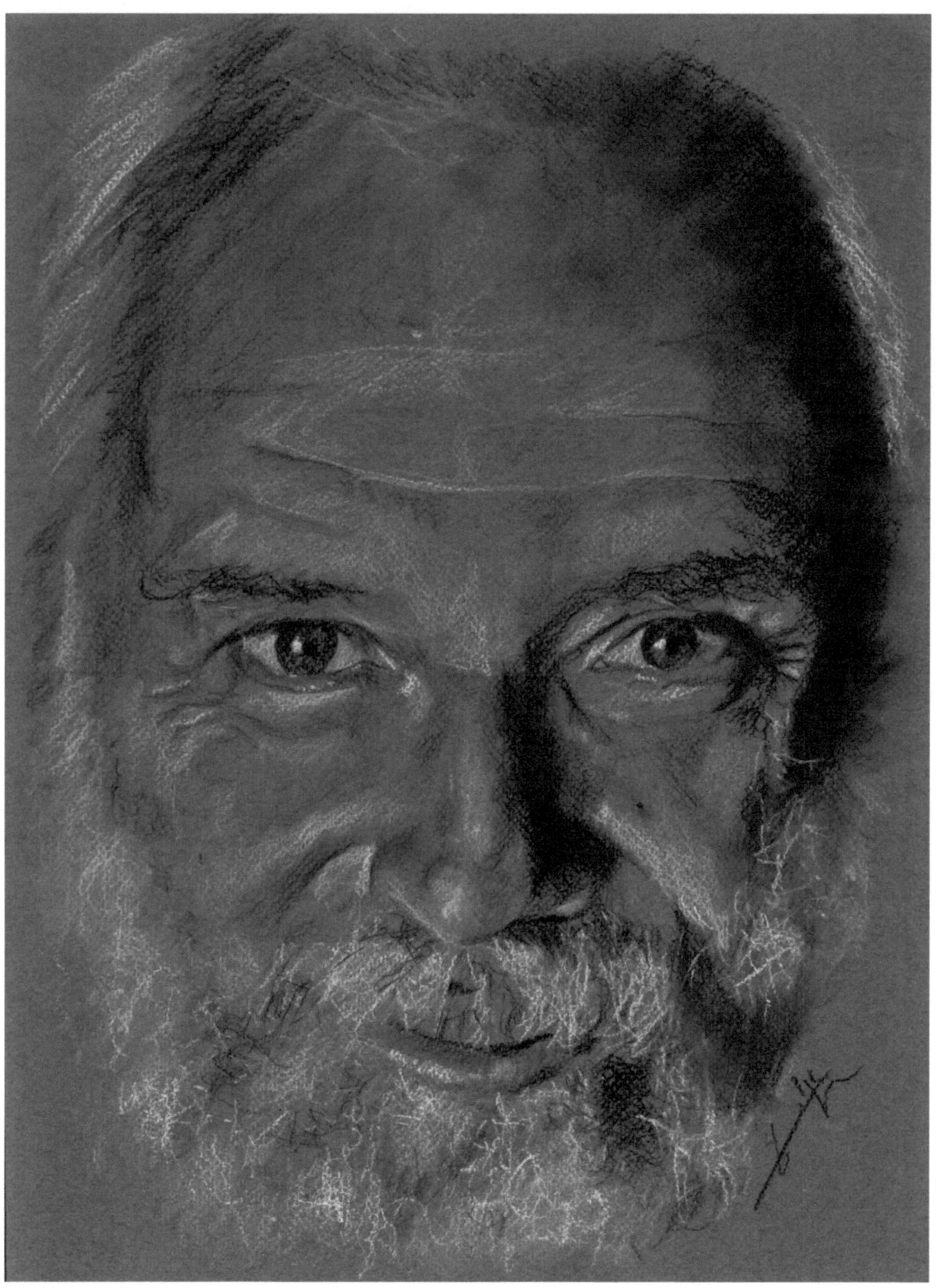

36

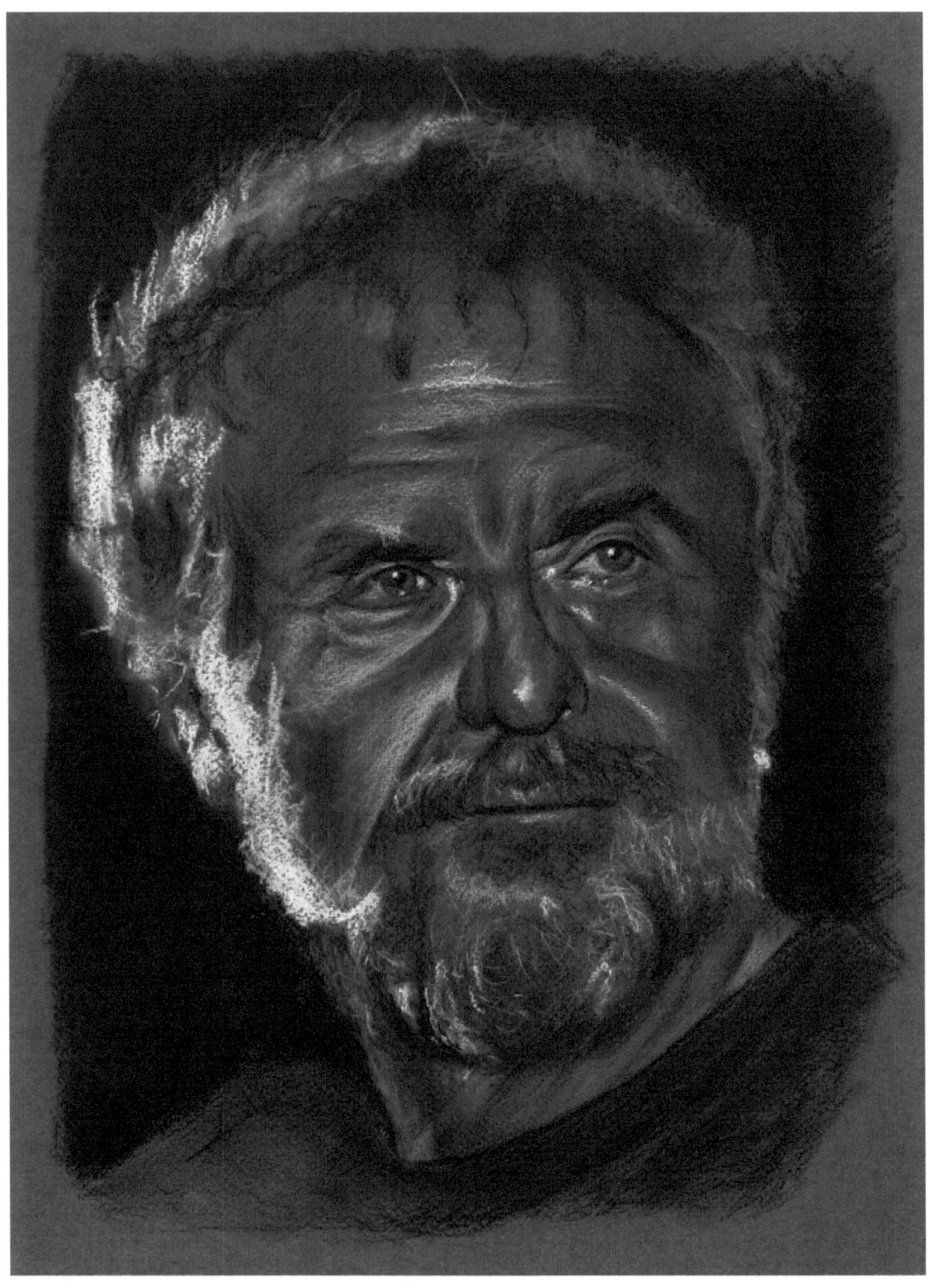

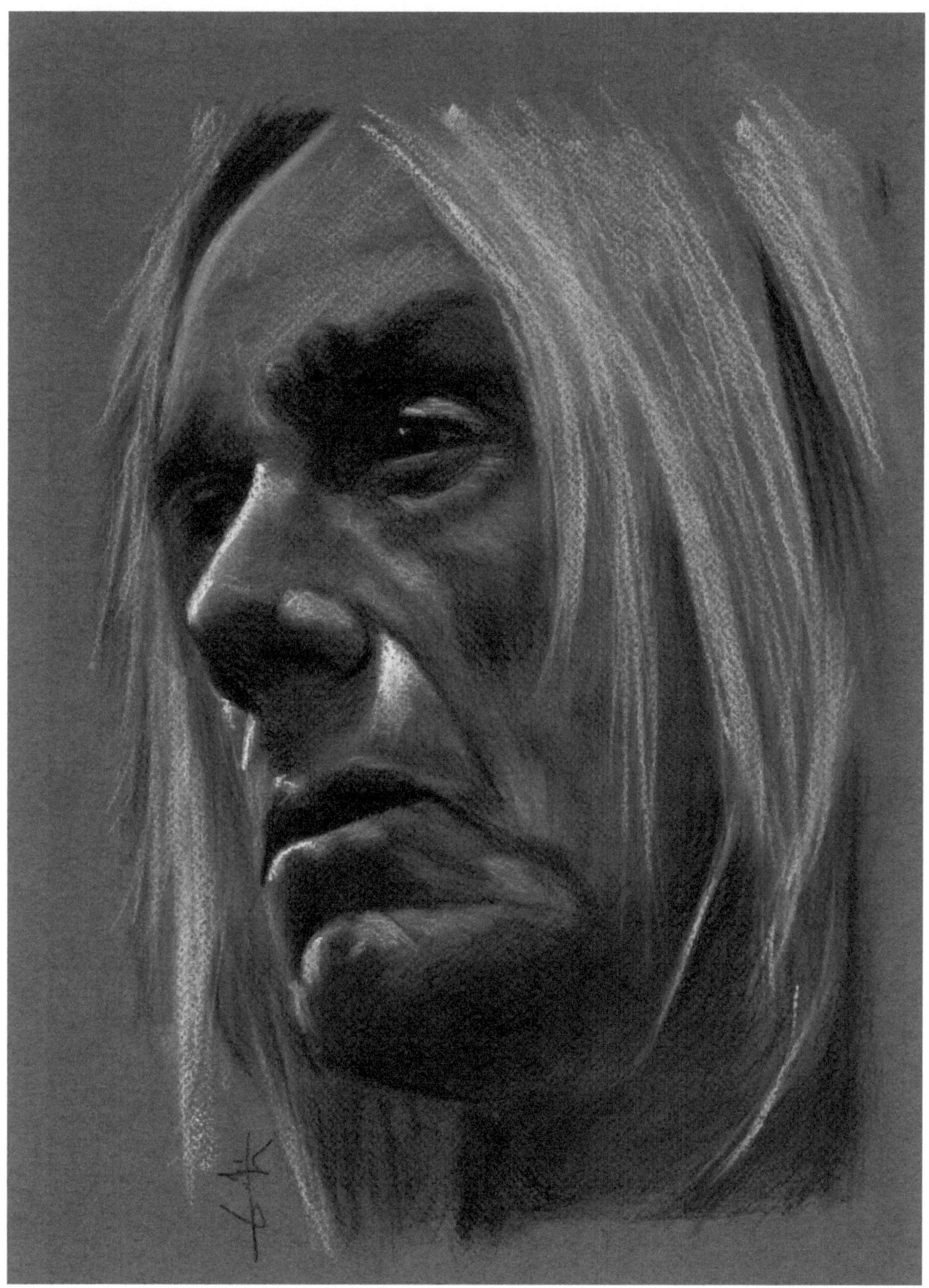

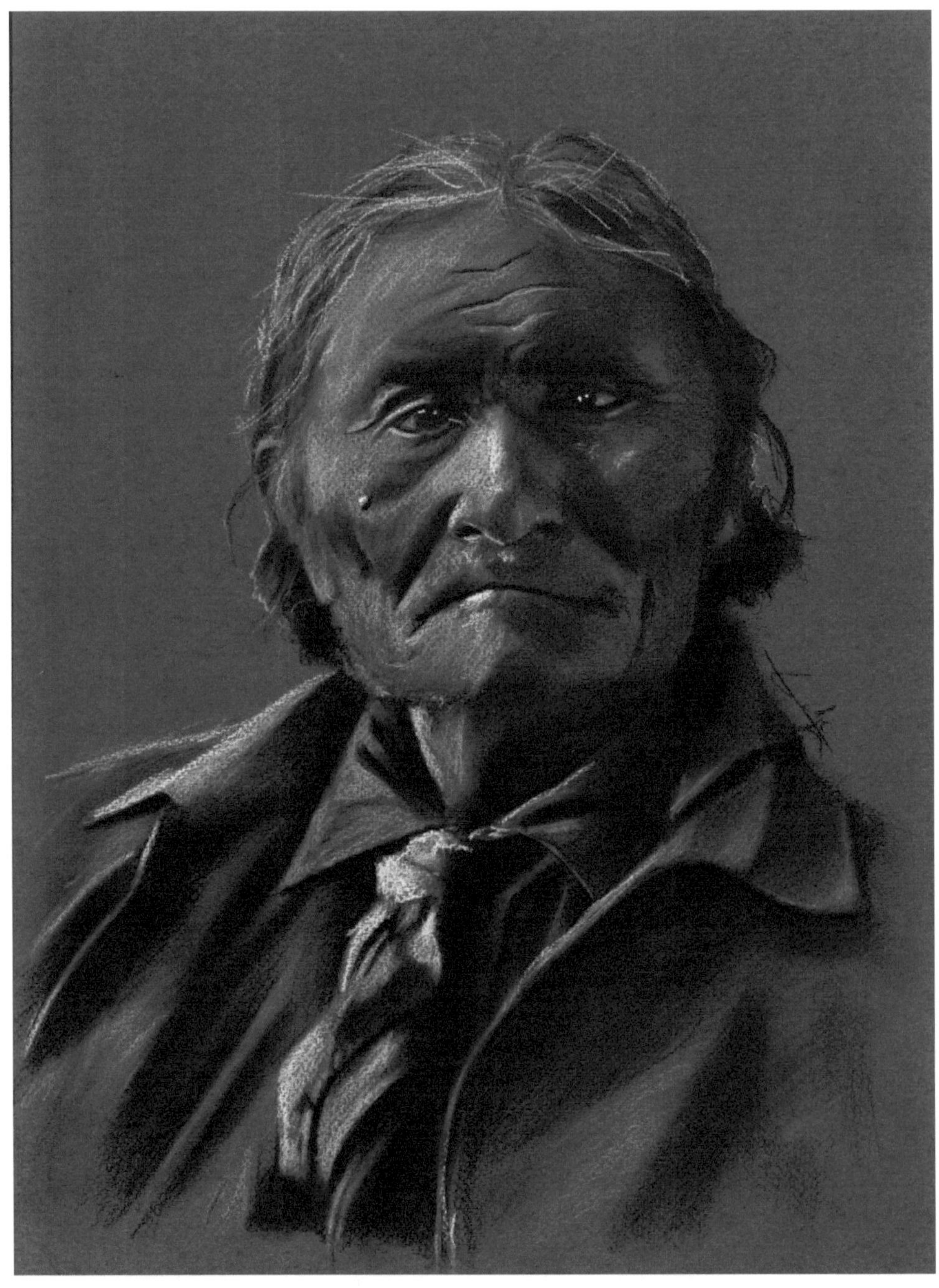

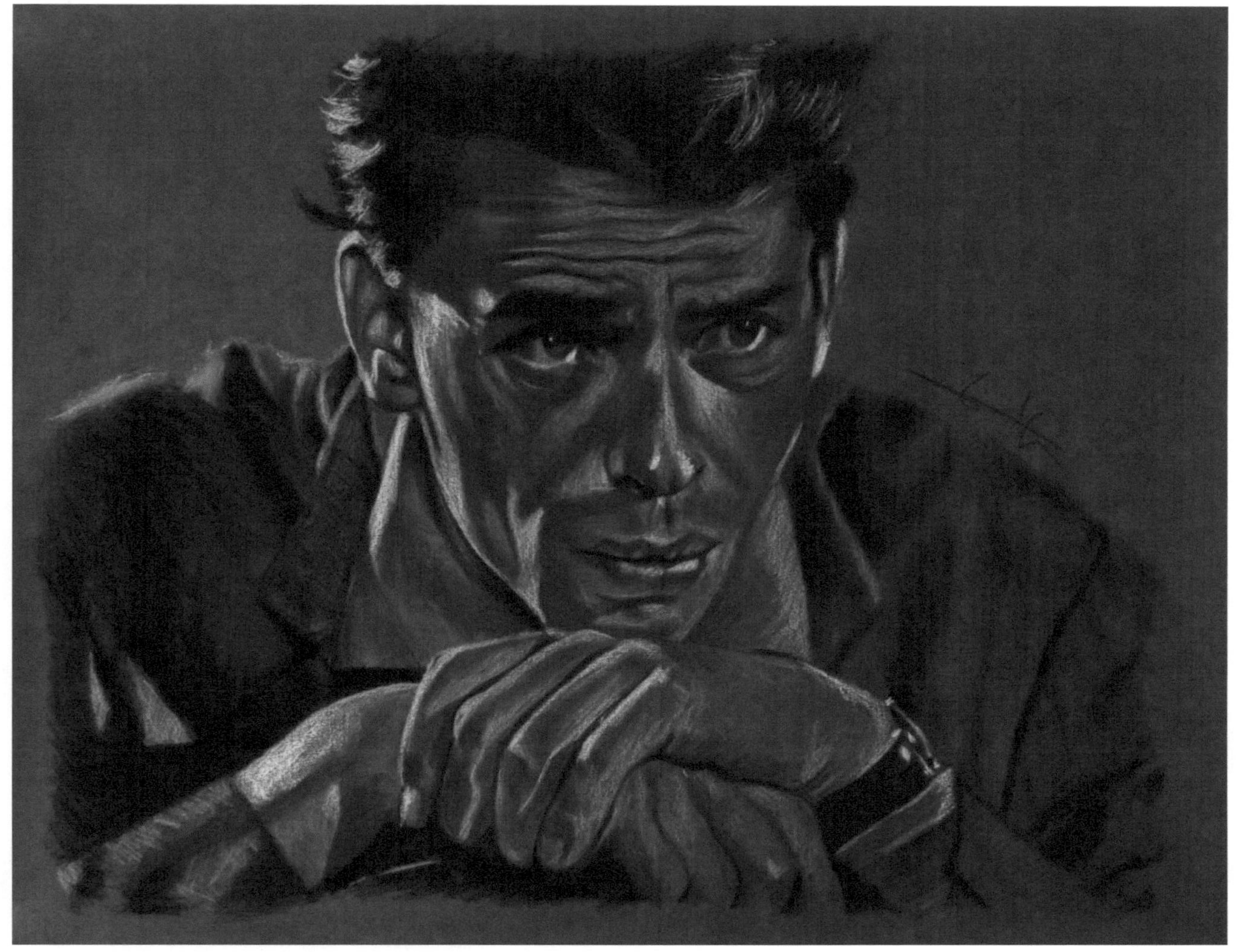

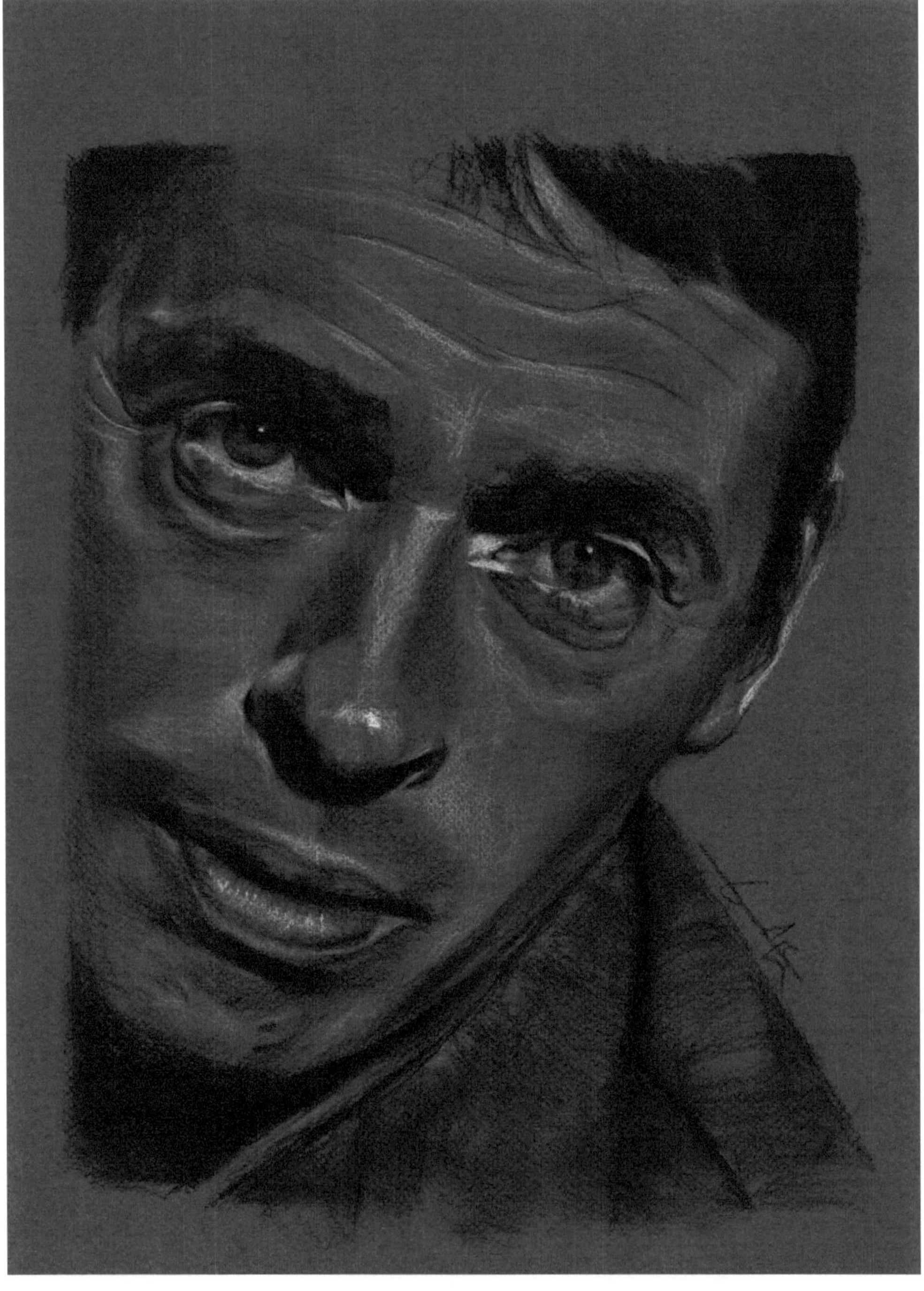

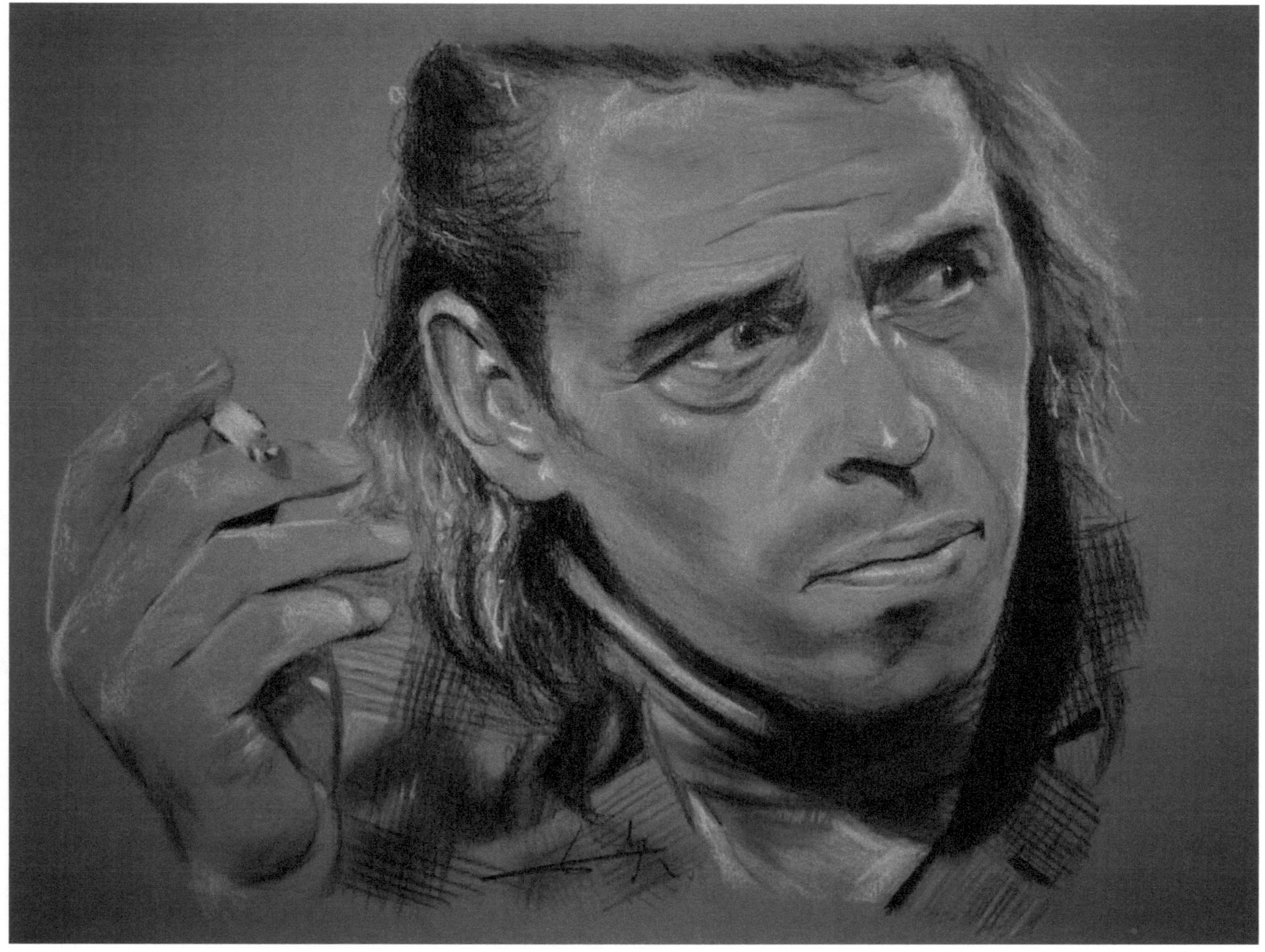

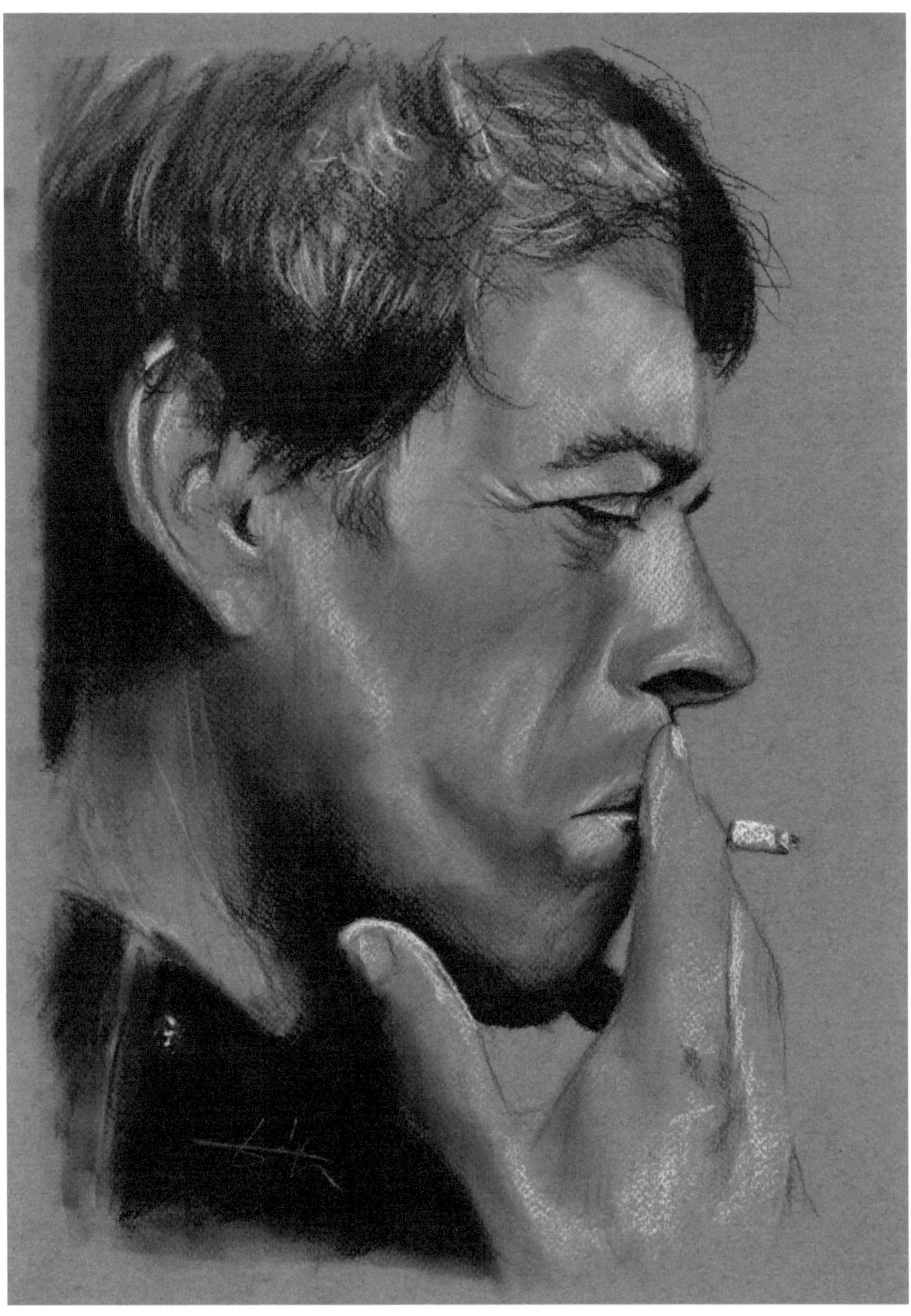

43

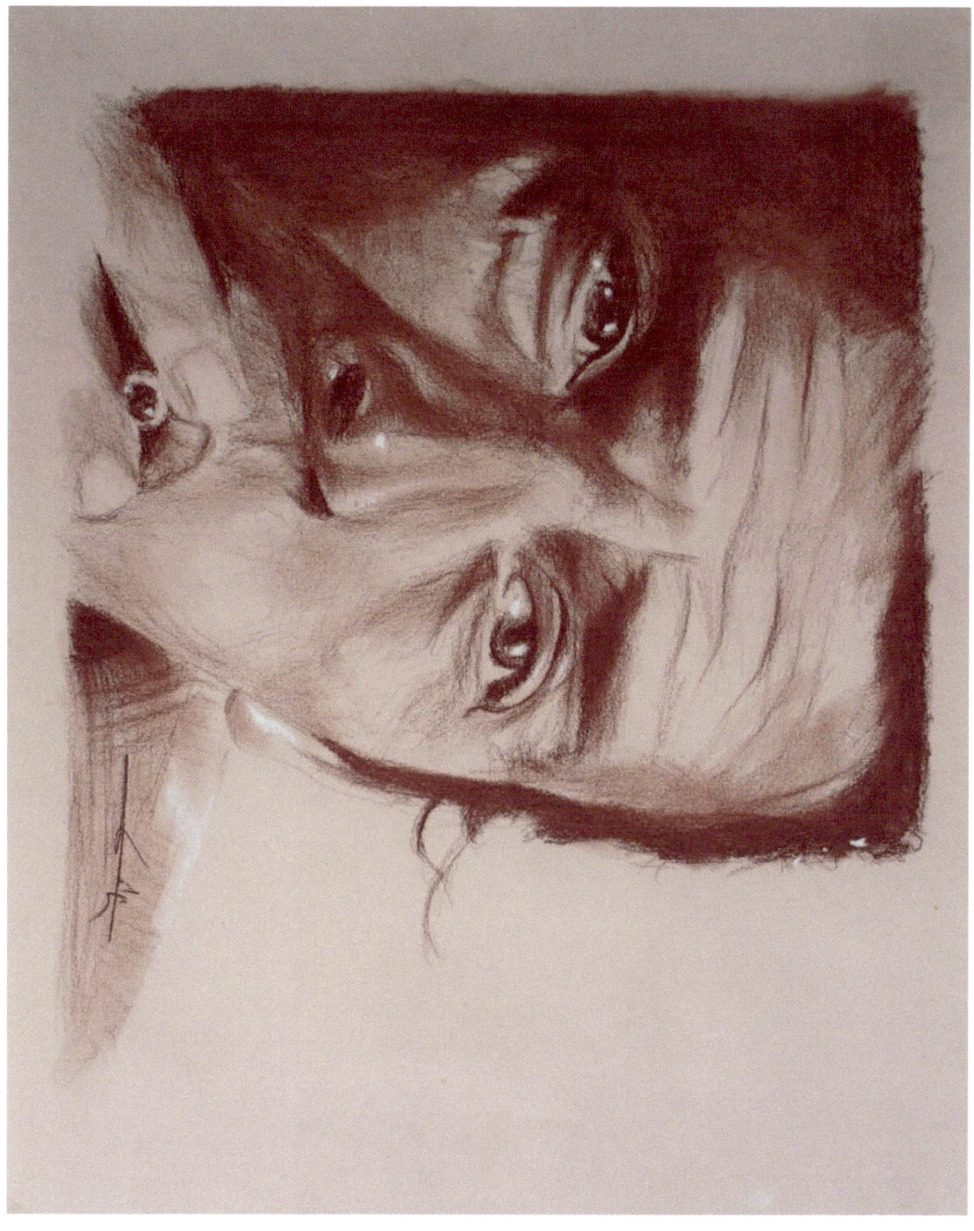

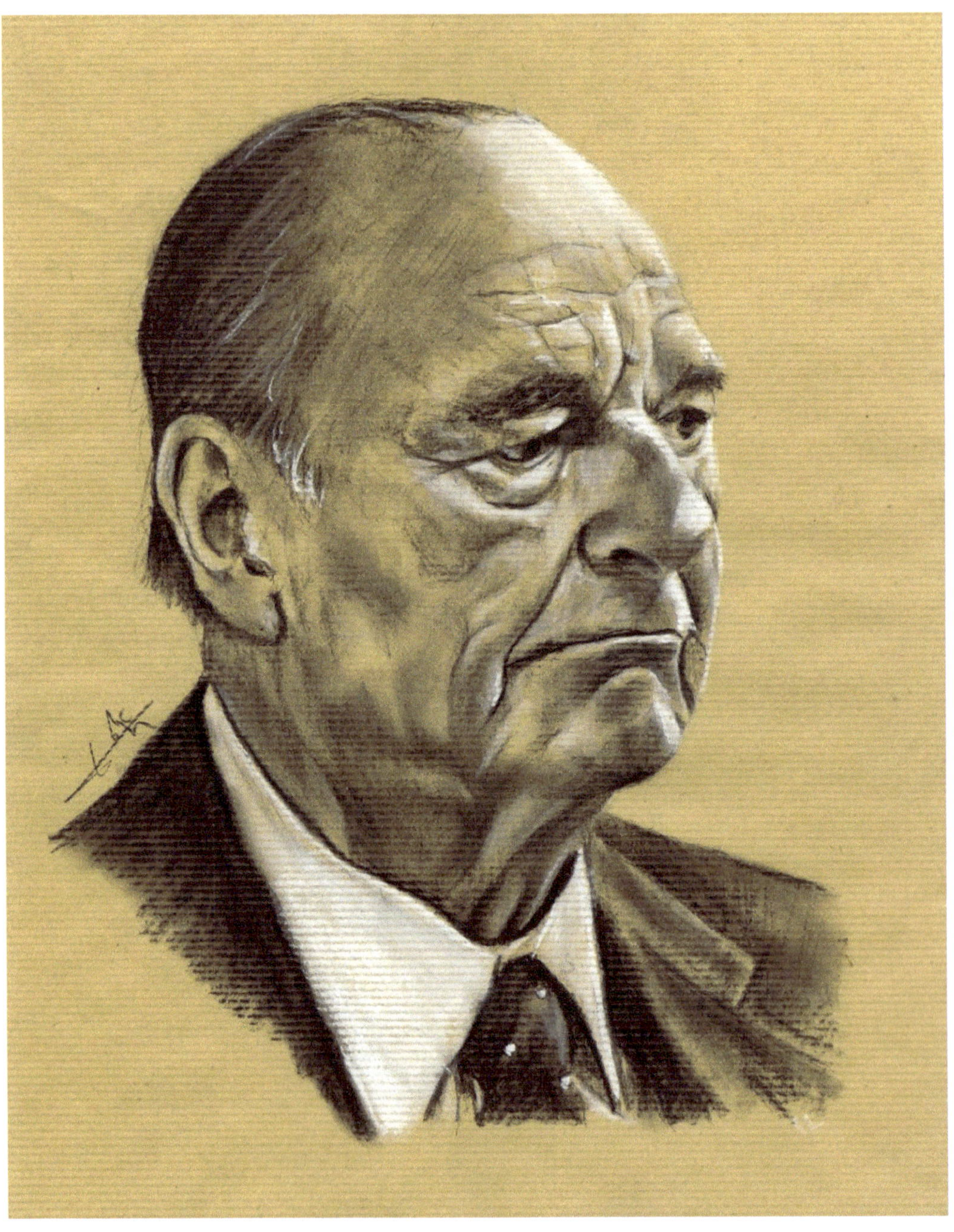

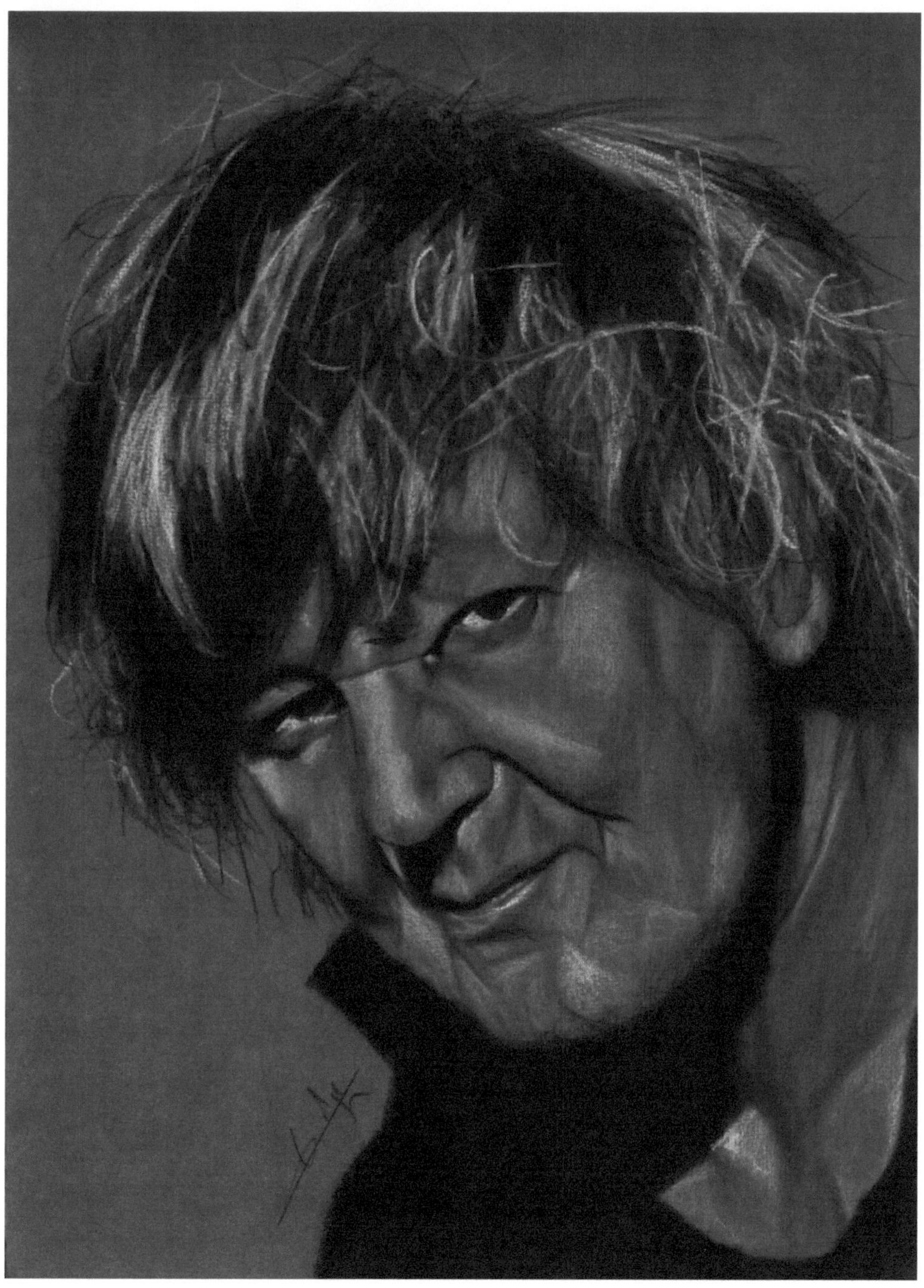

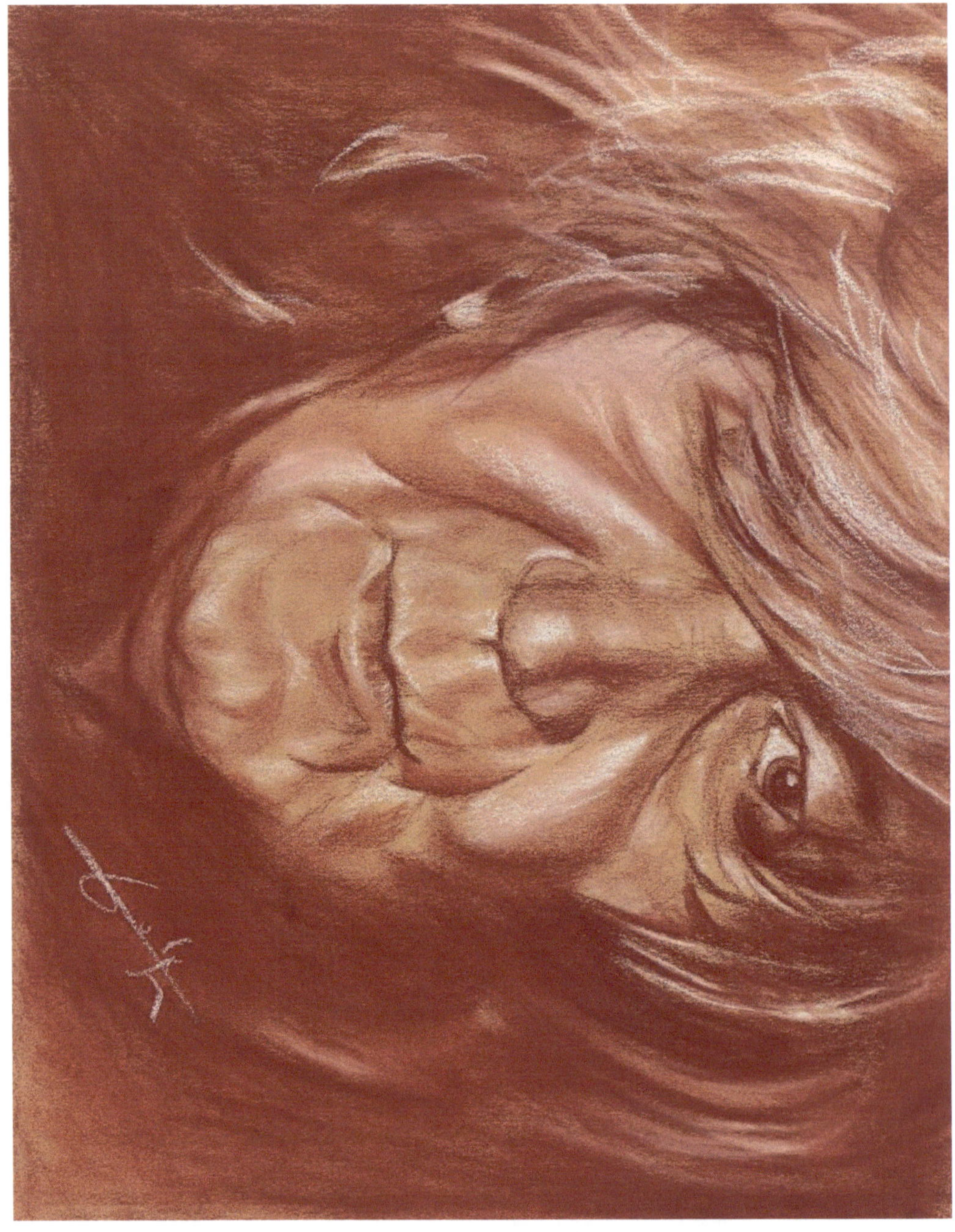

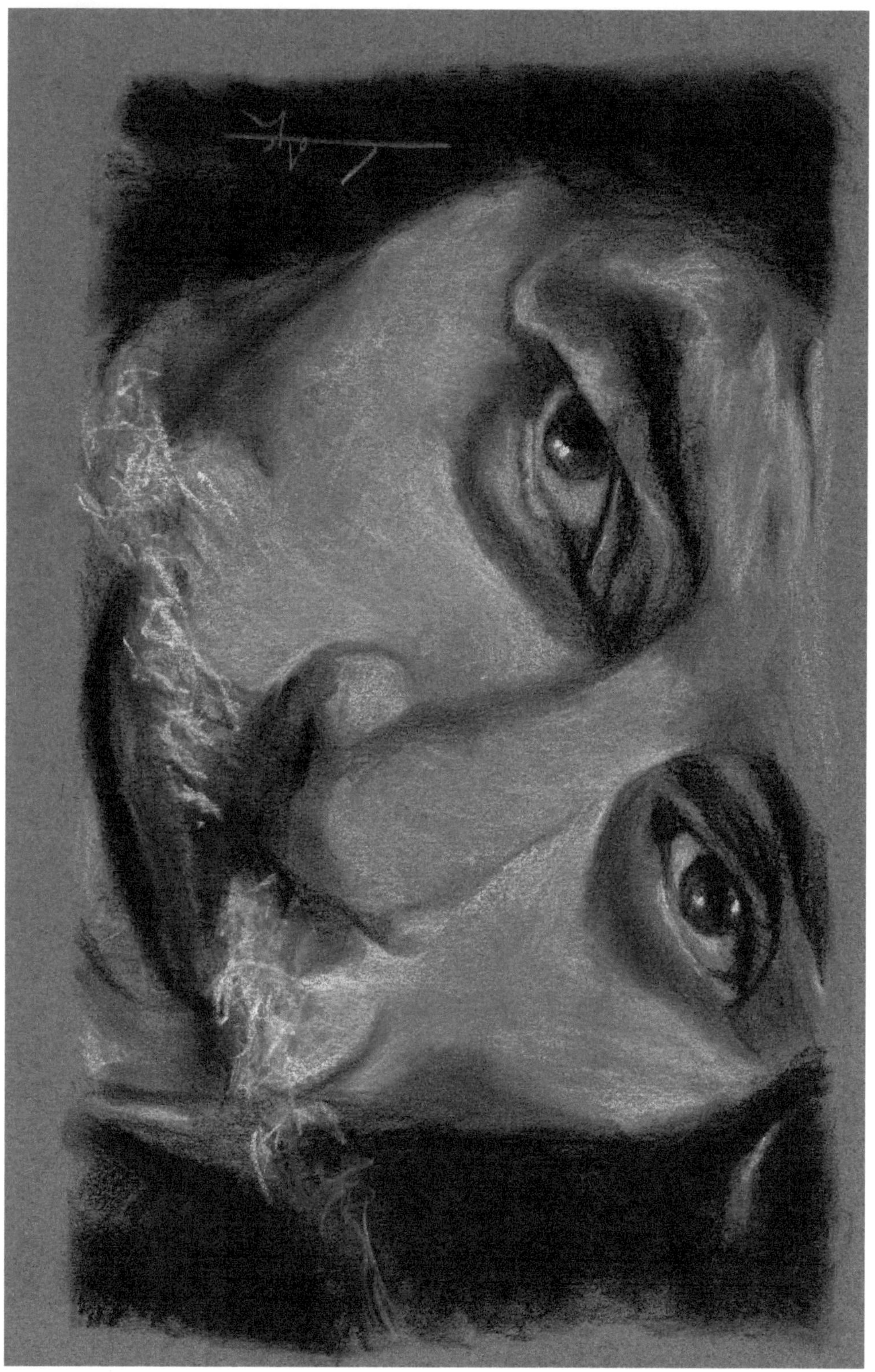

48

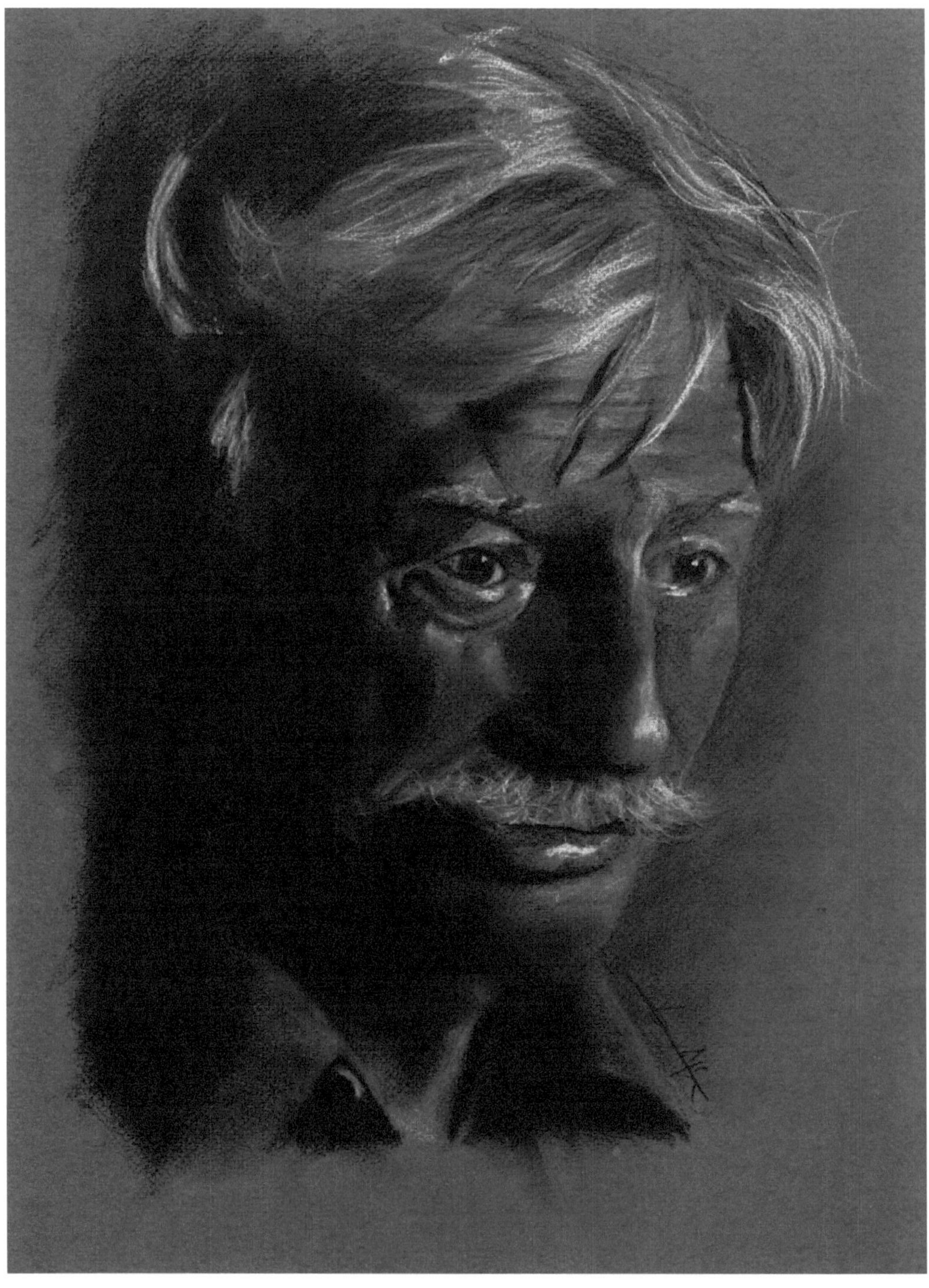

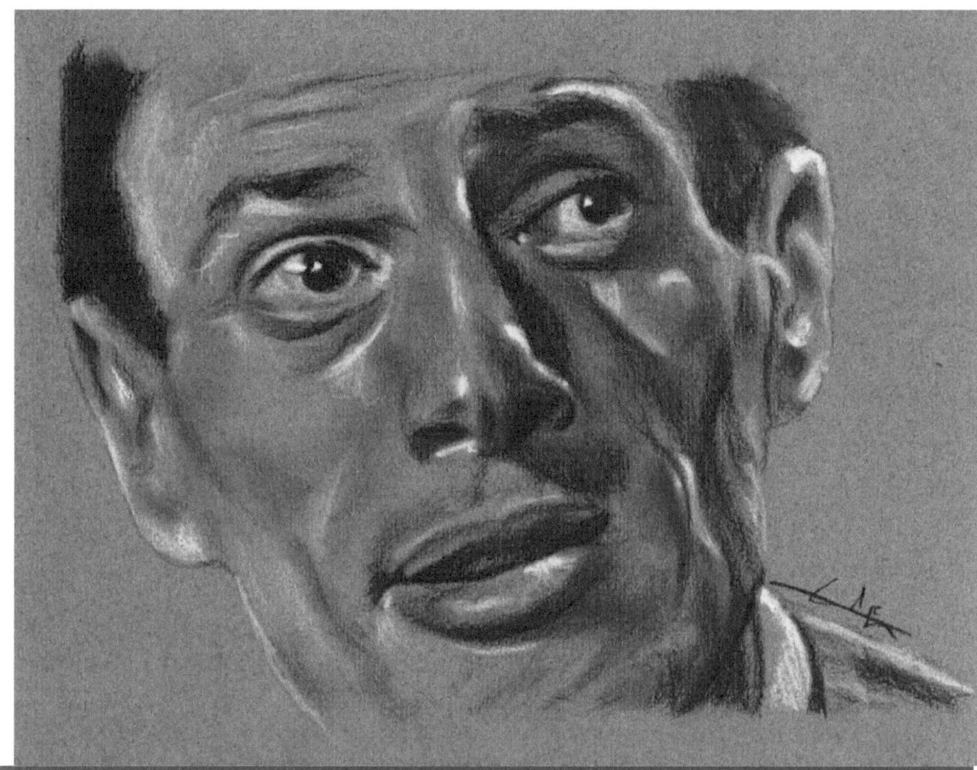

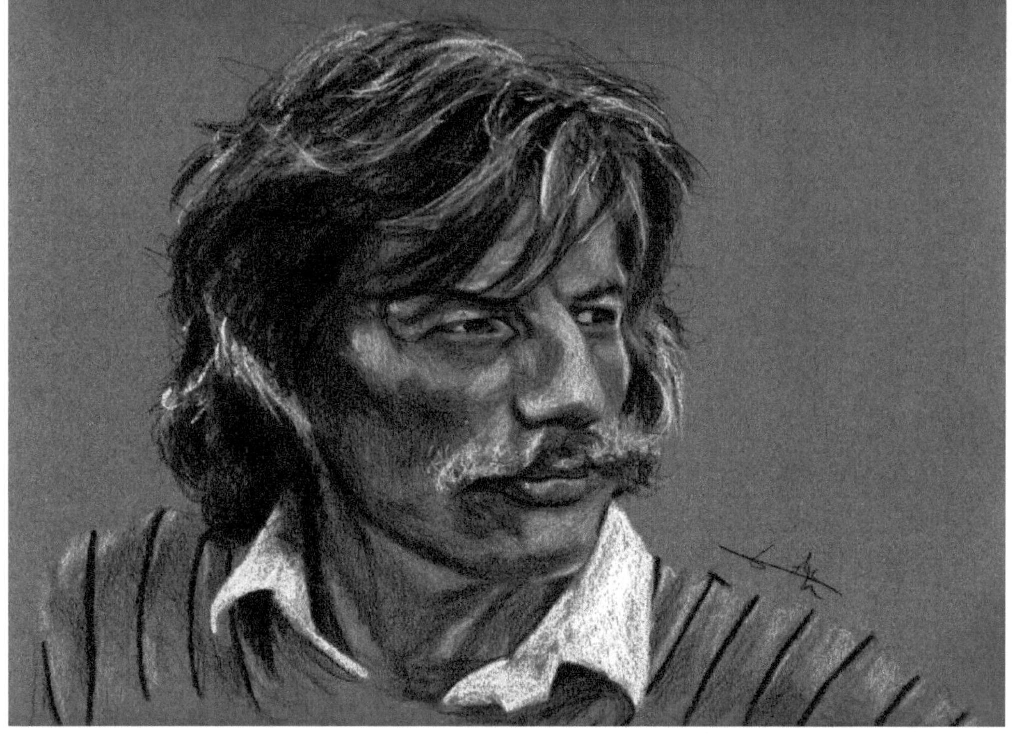

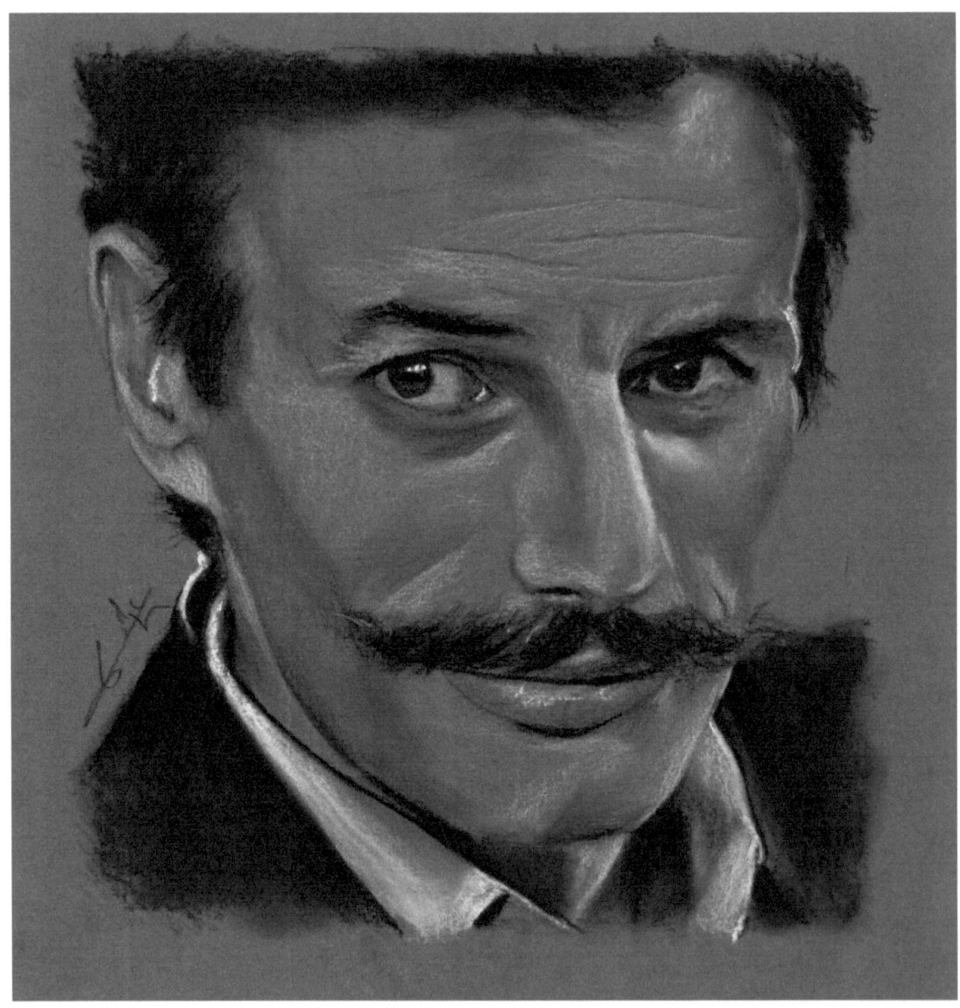

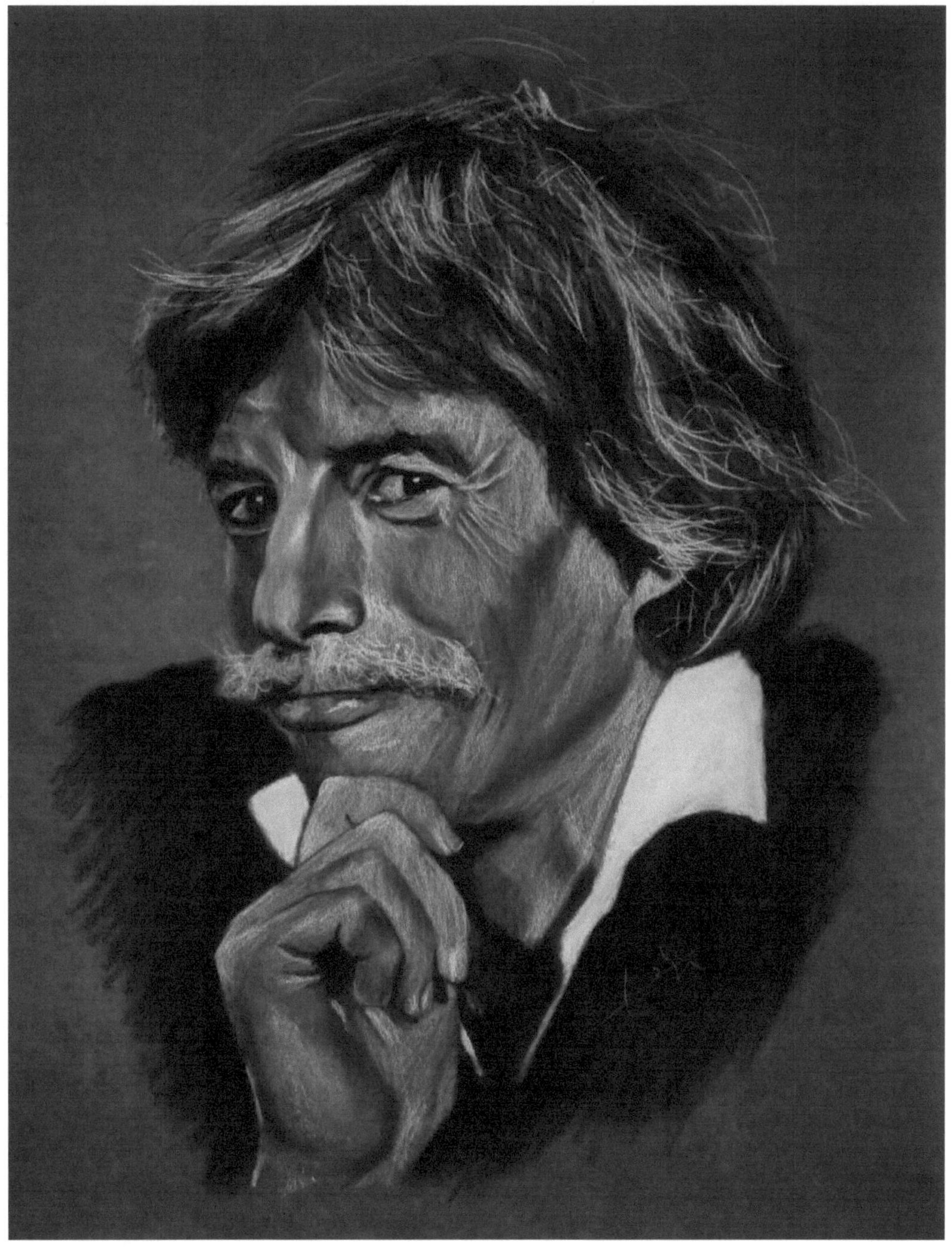

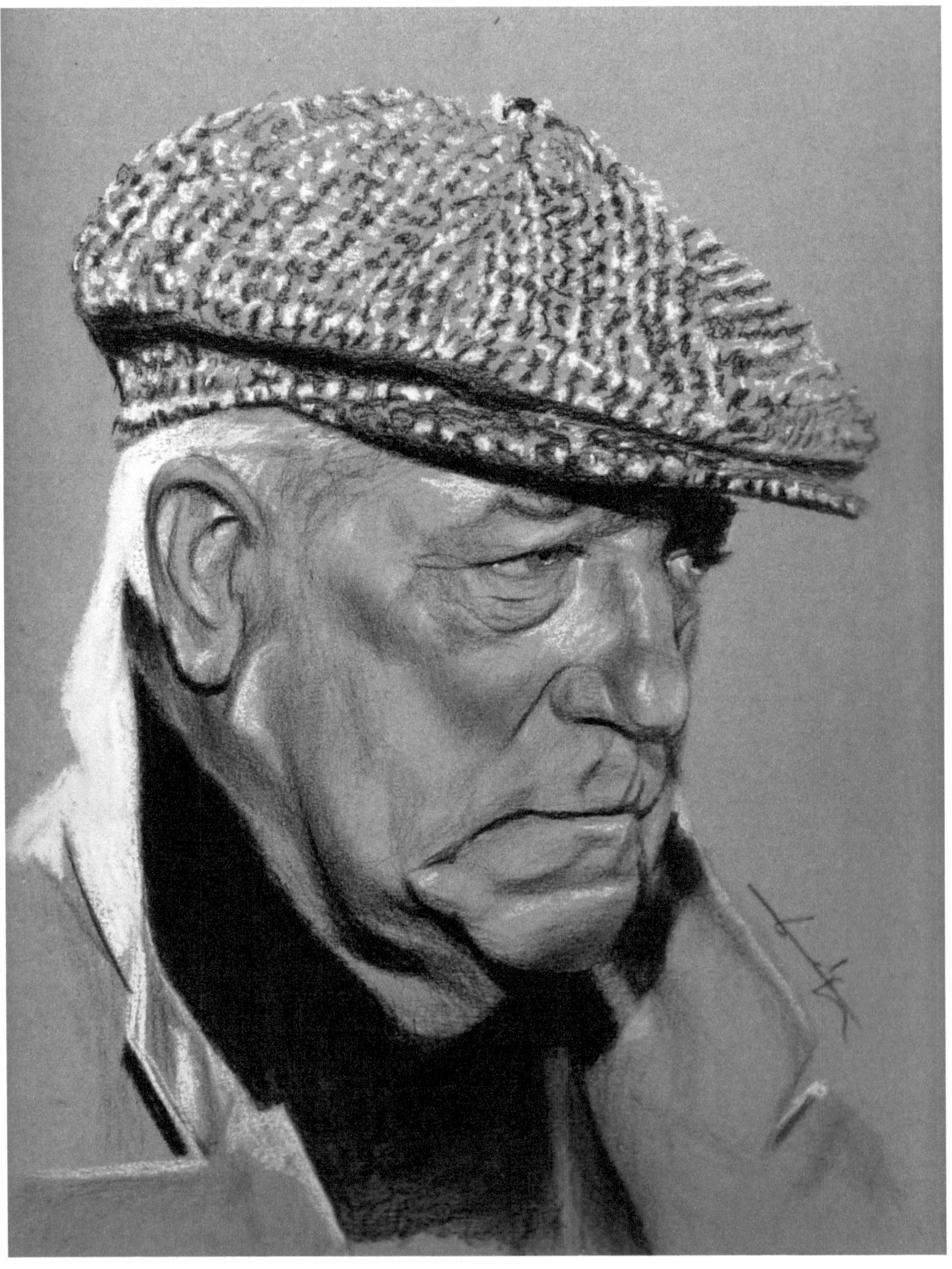

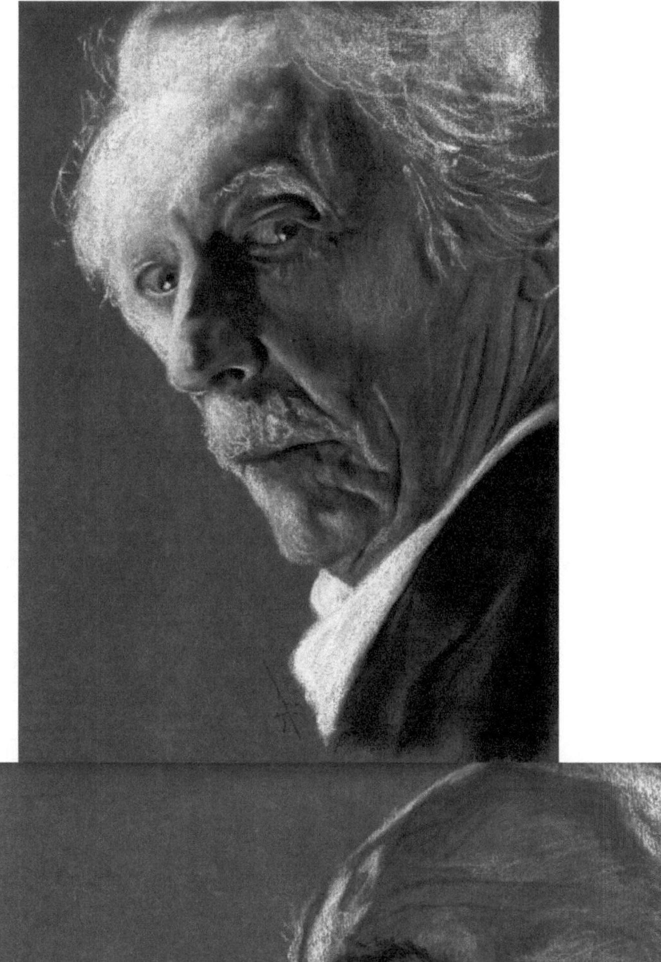

54

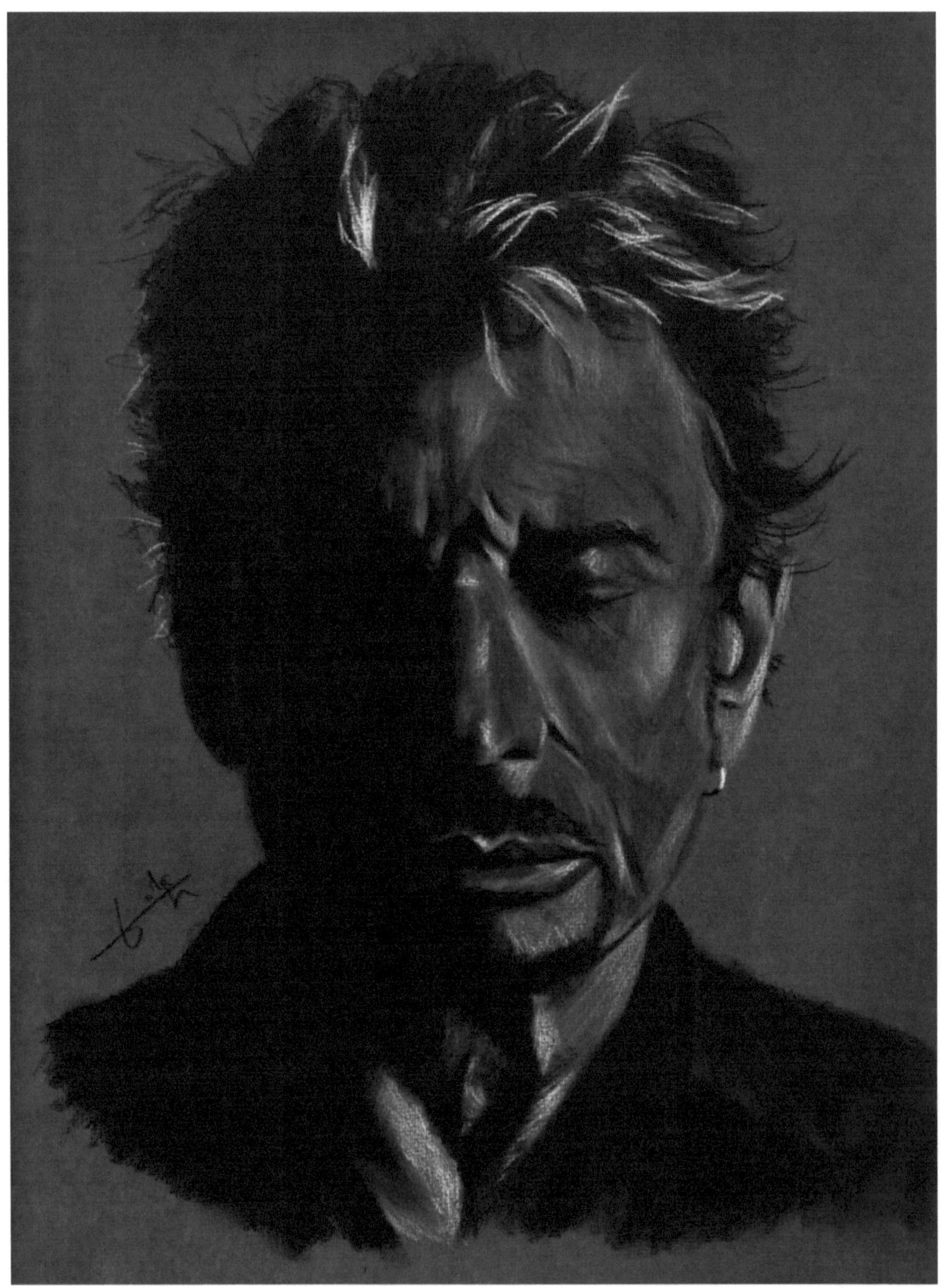

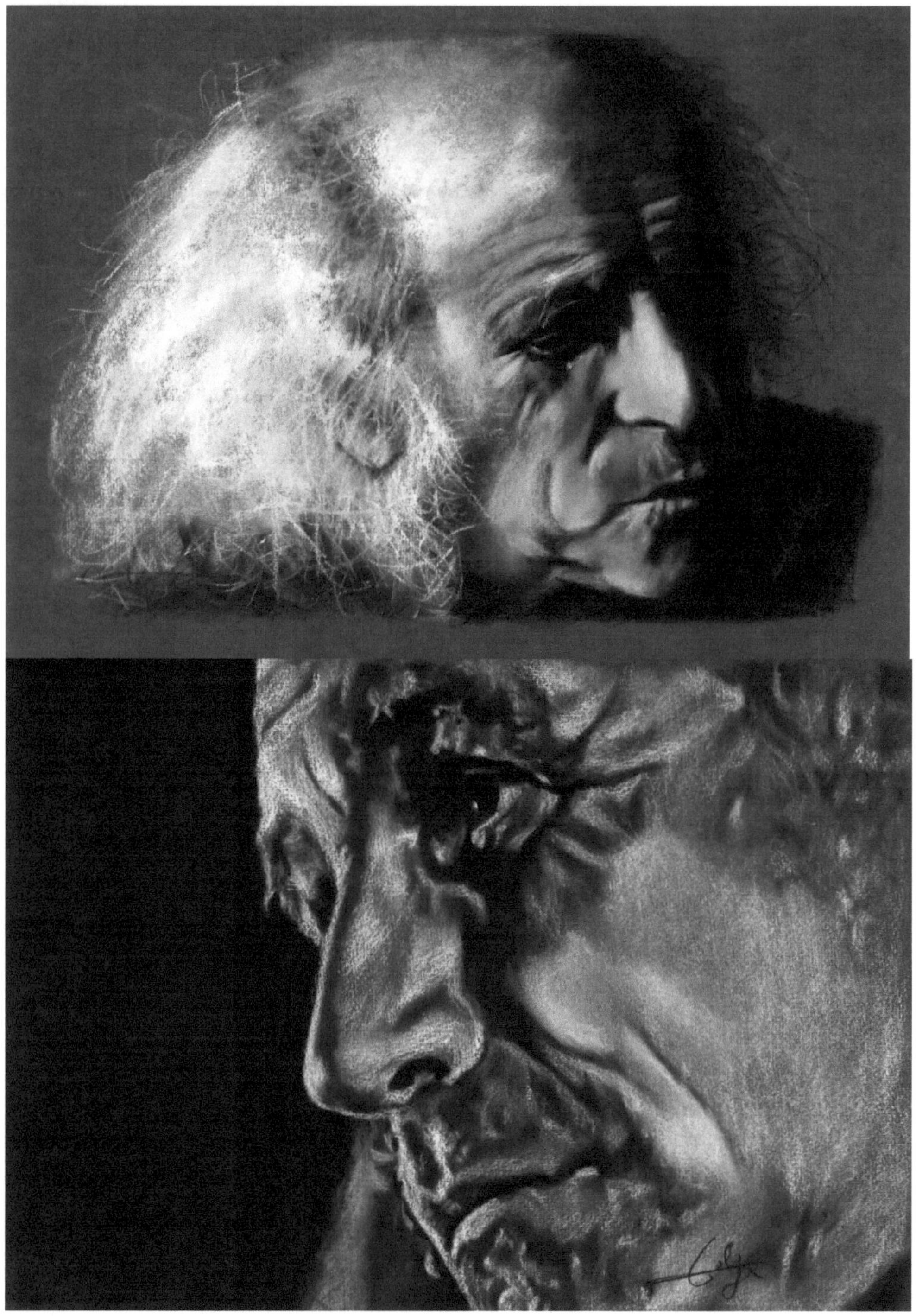

56

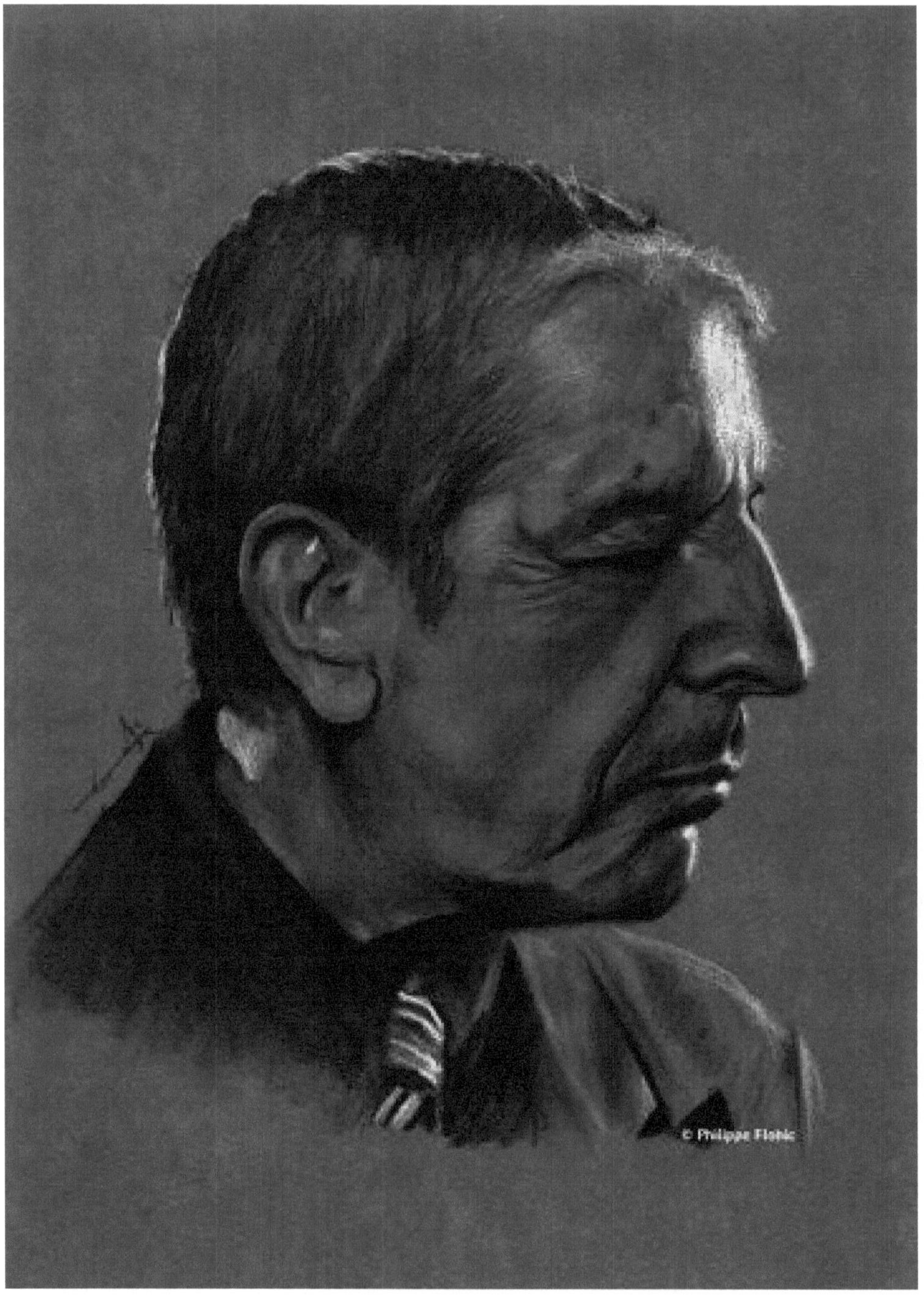

57

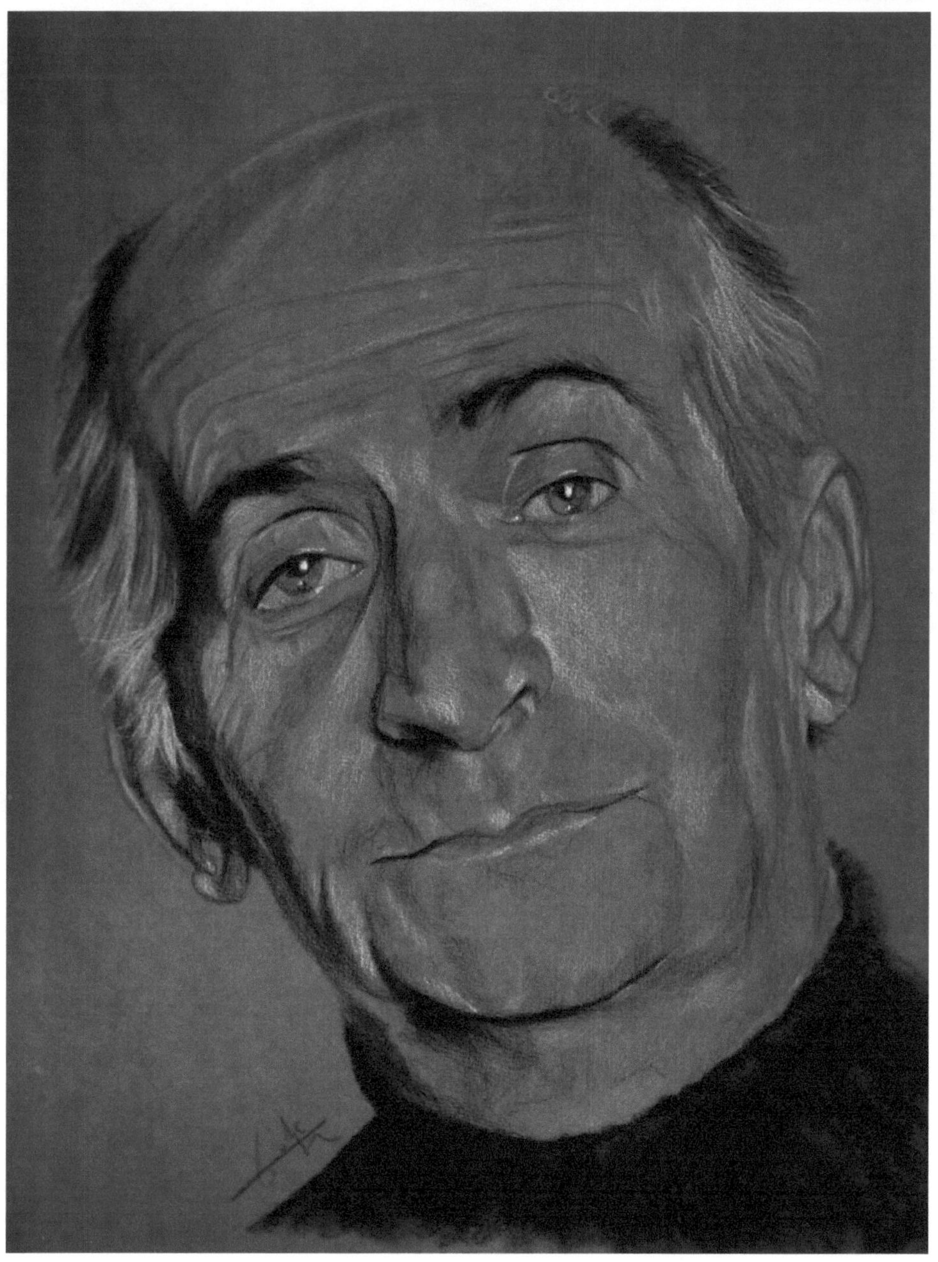

58

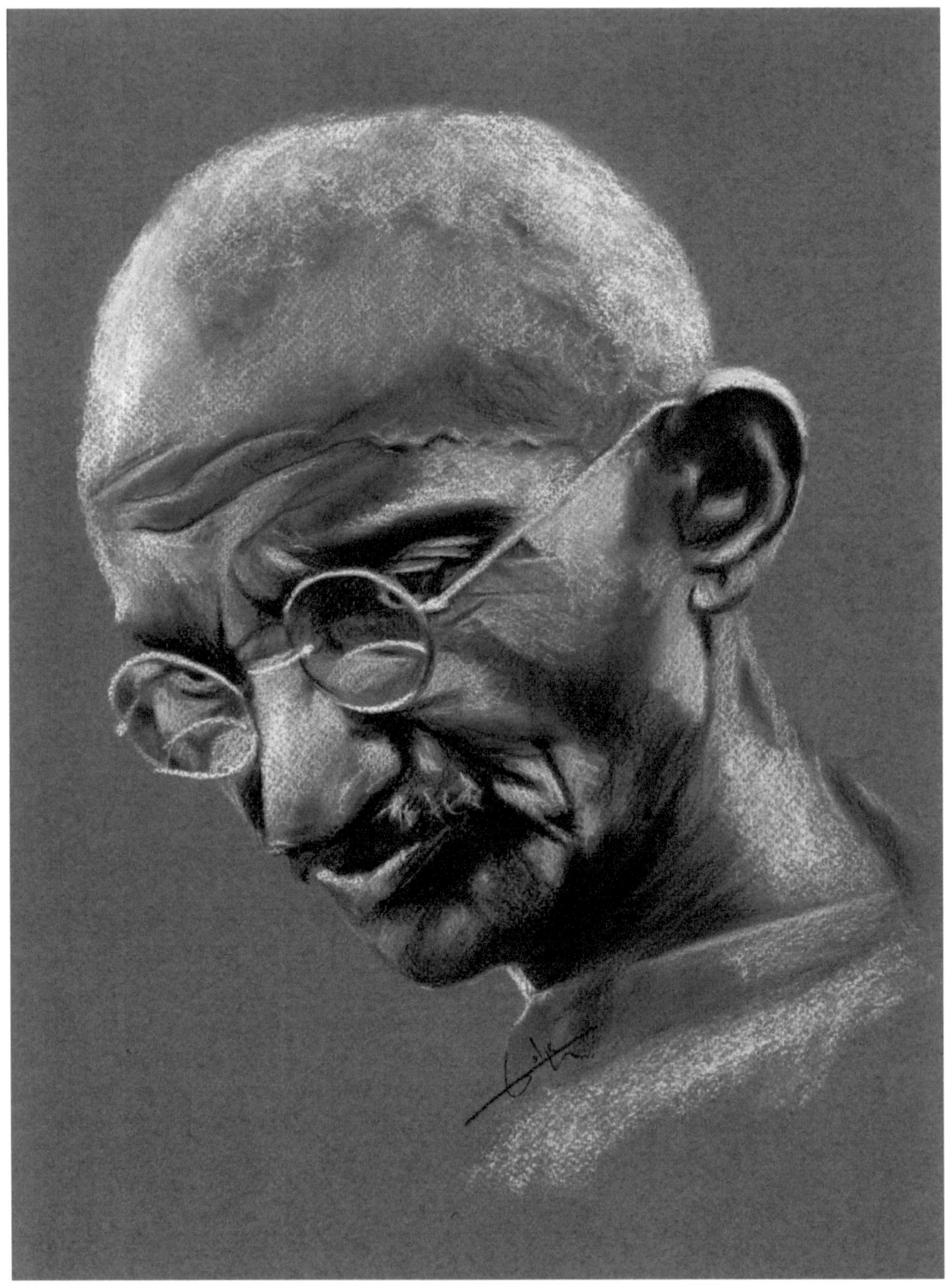

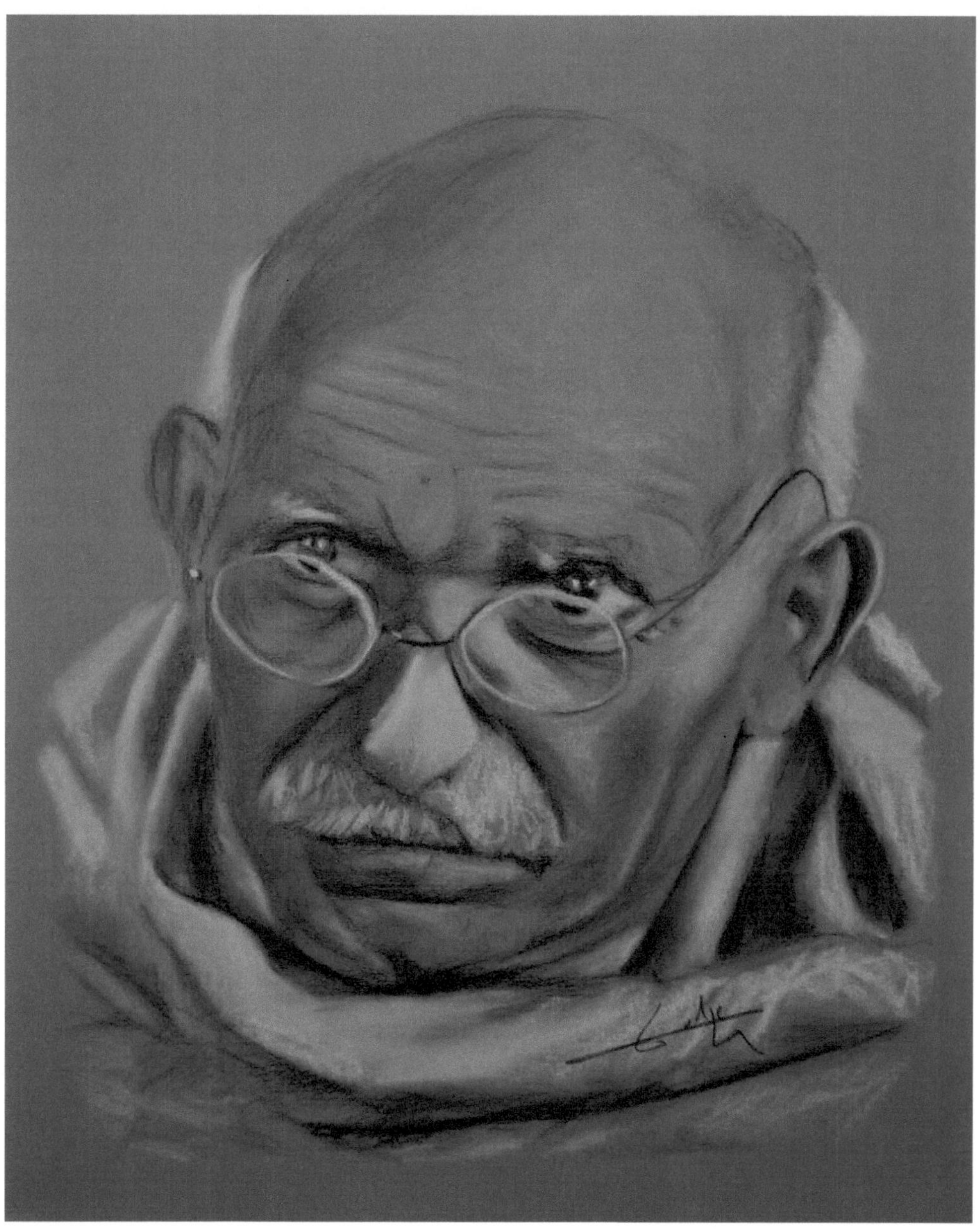

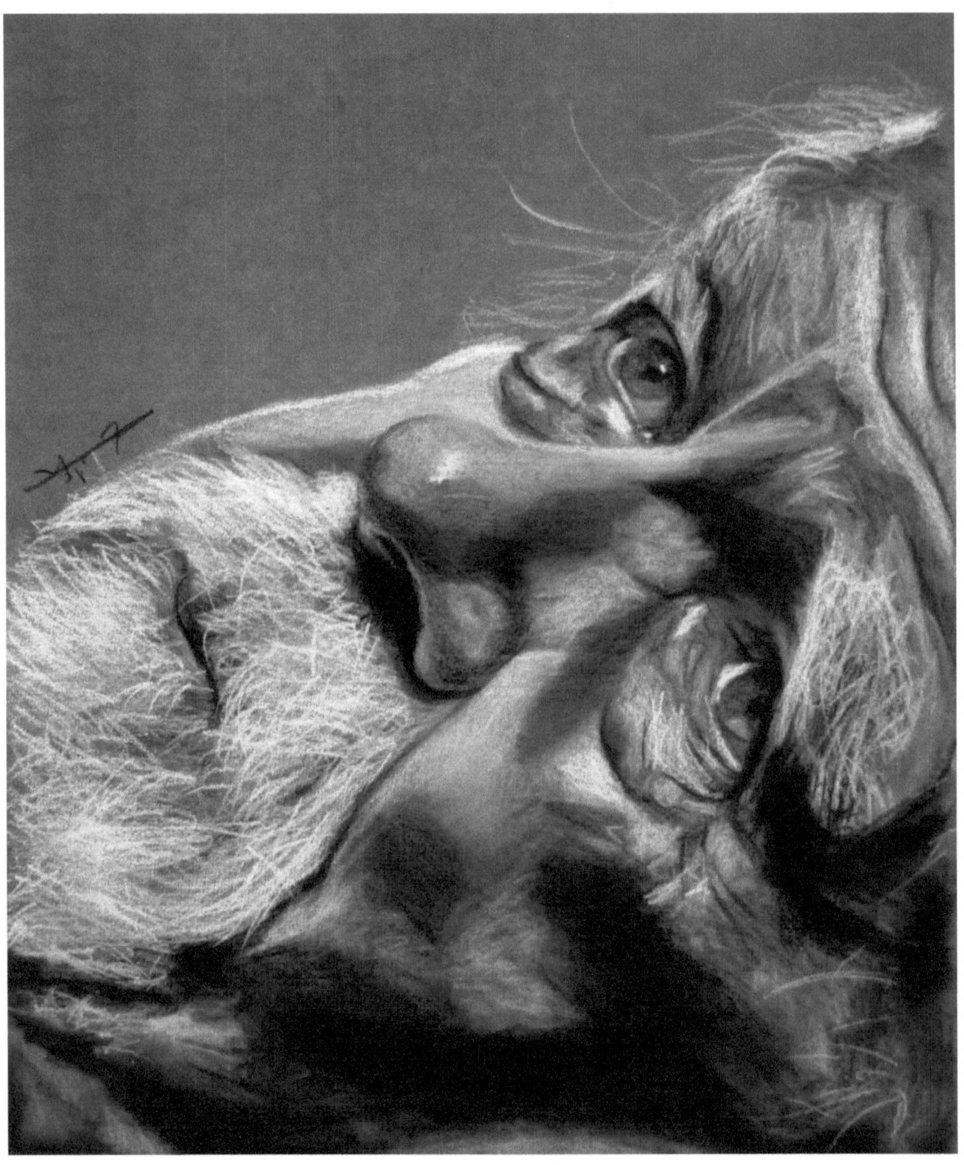

61

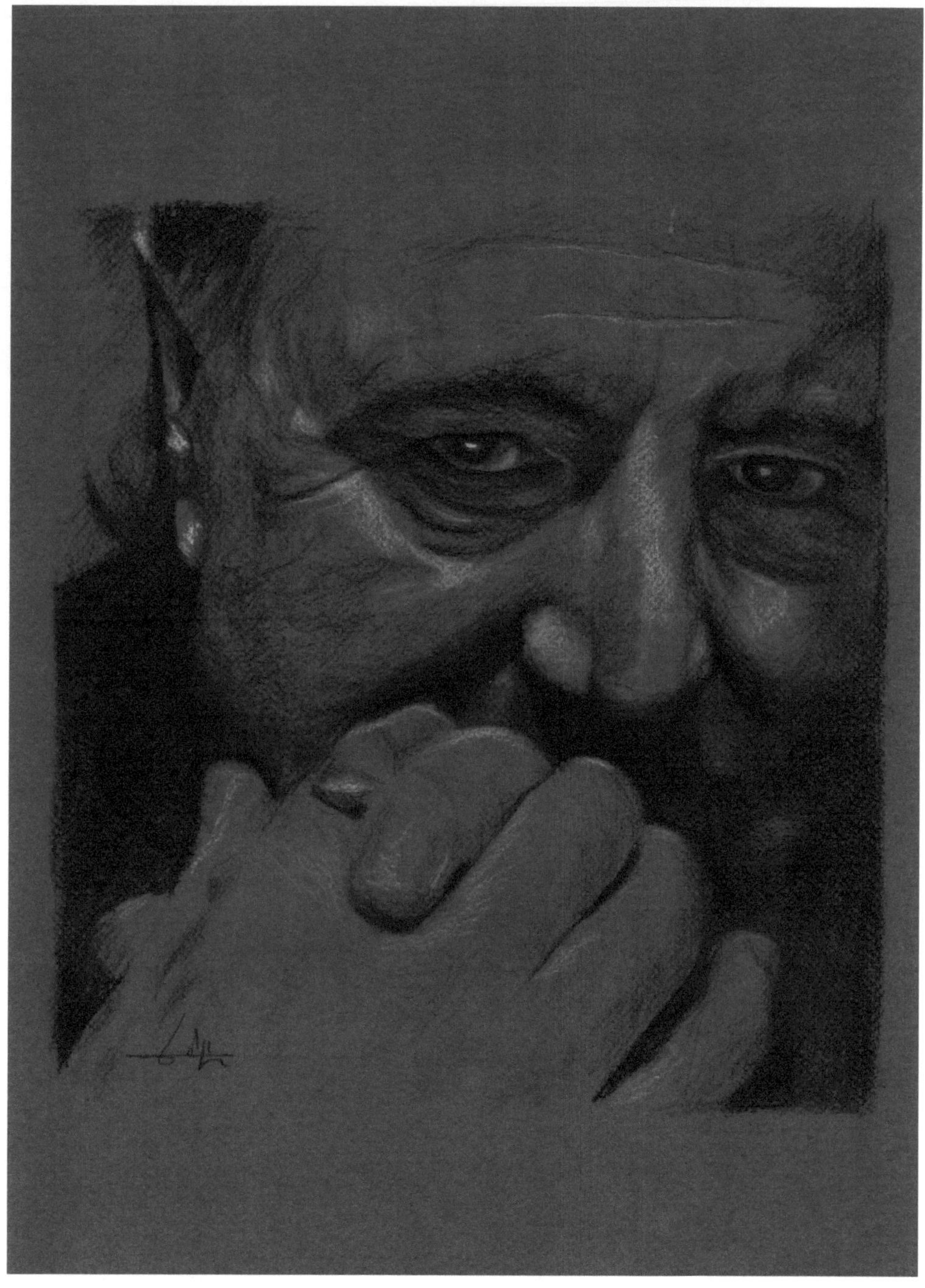

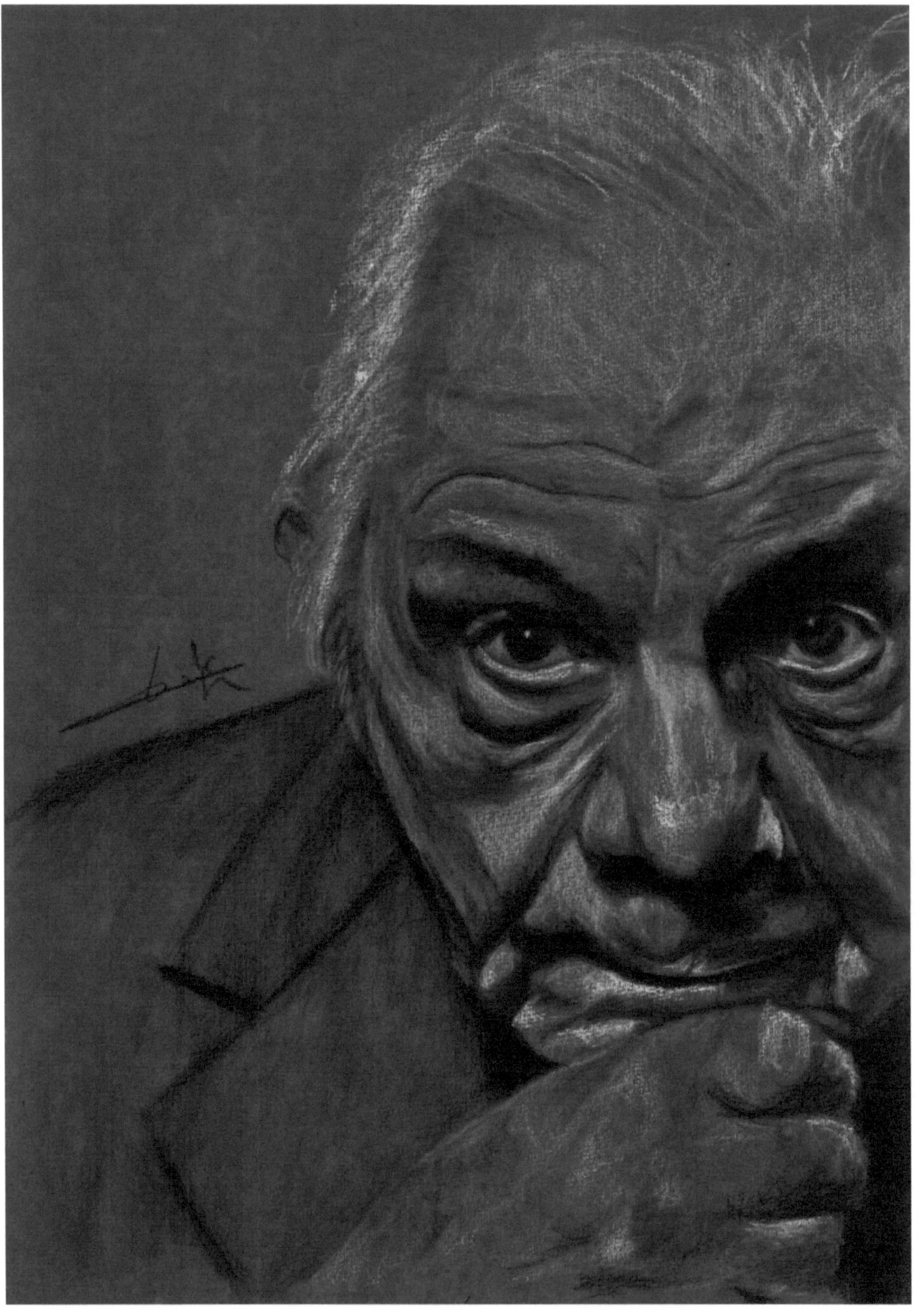

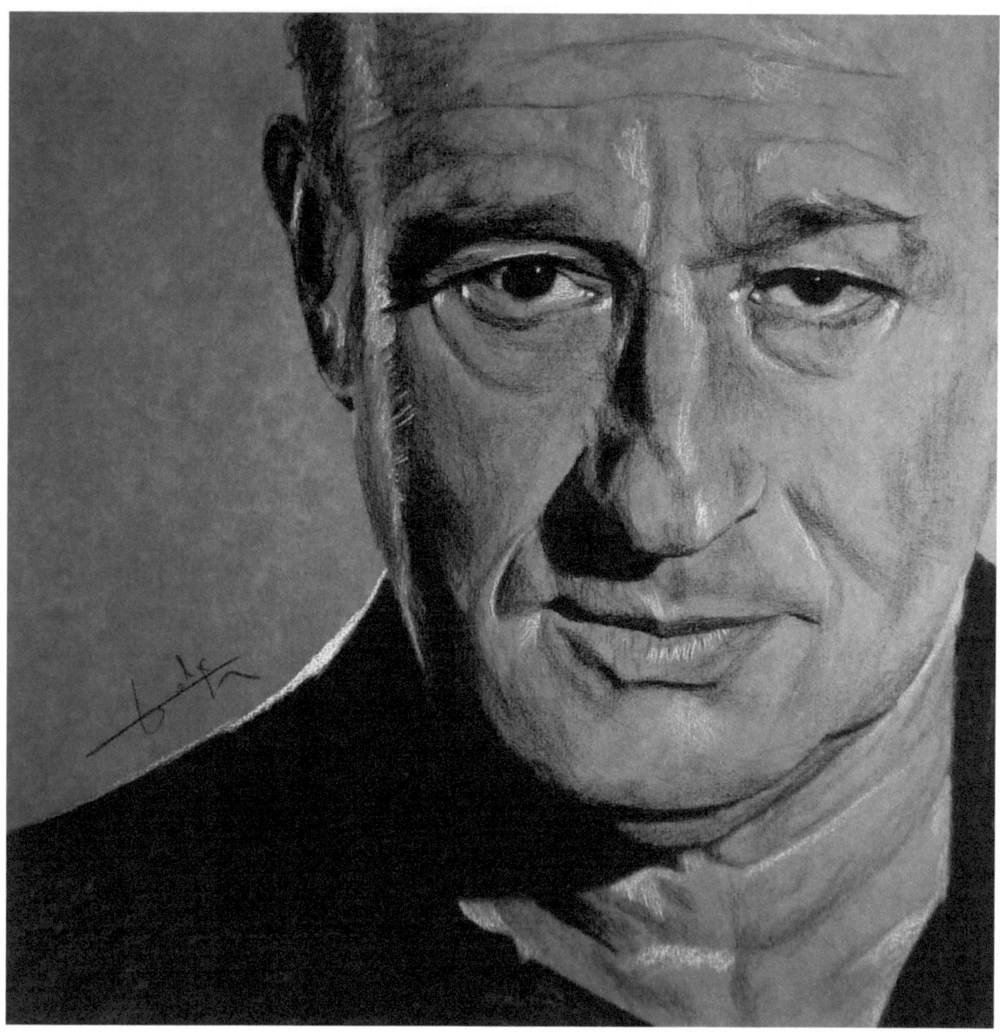

64

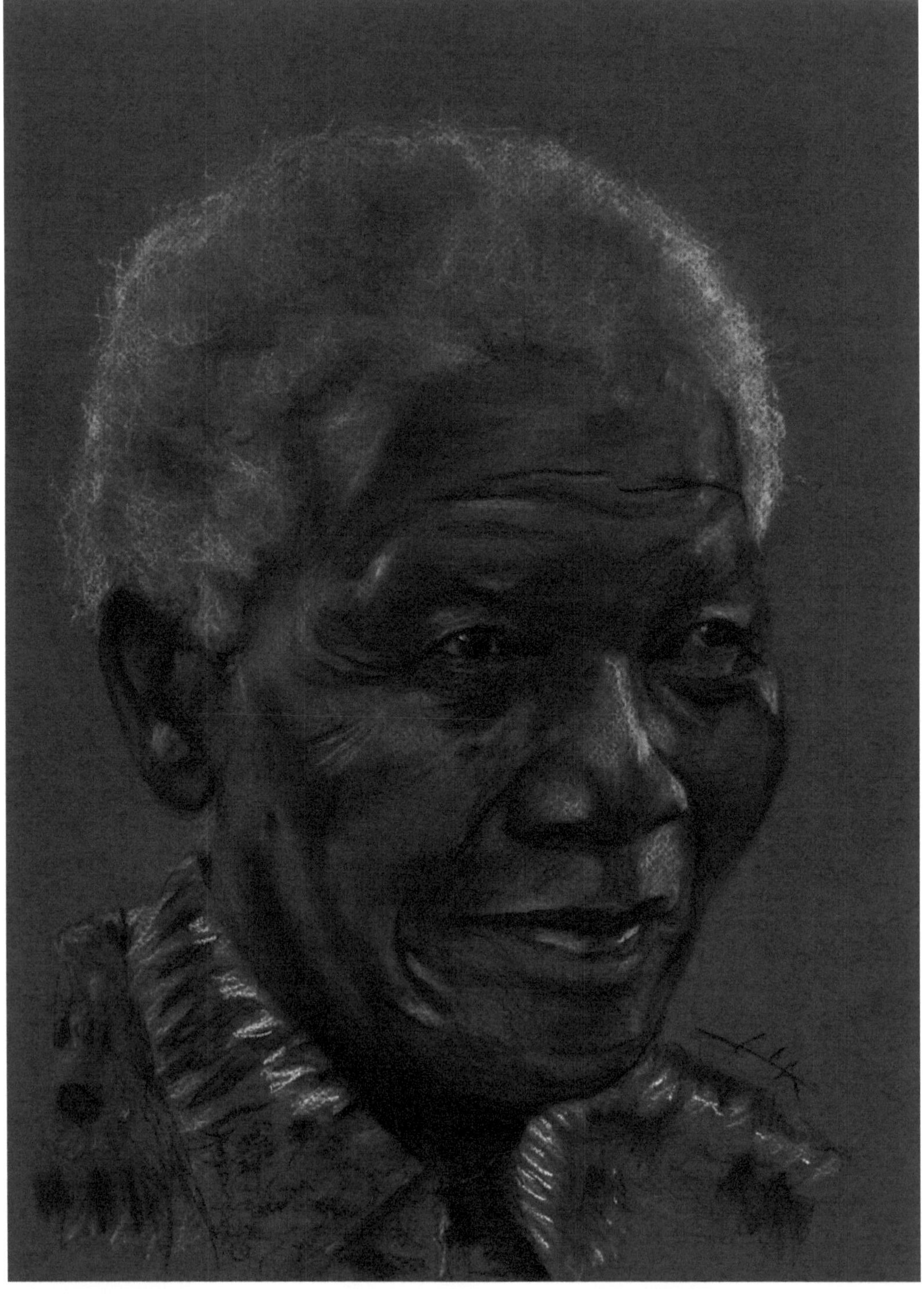

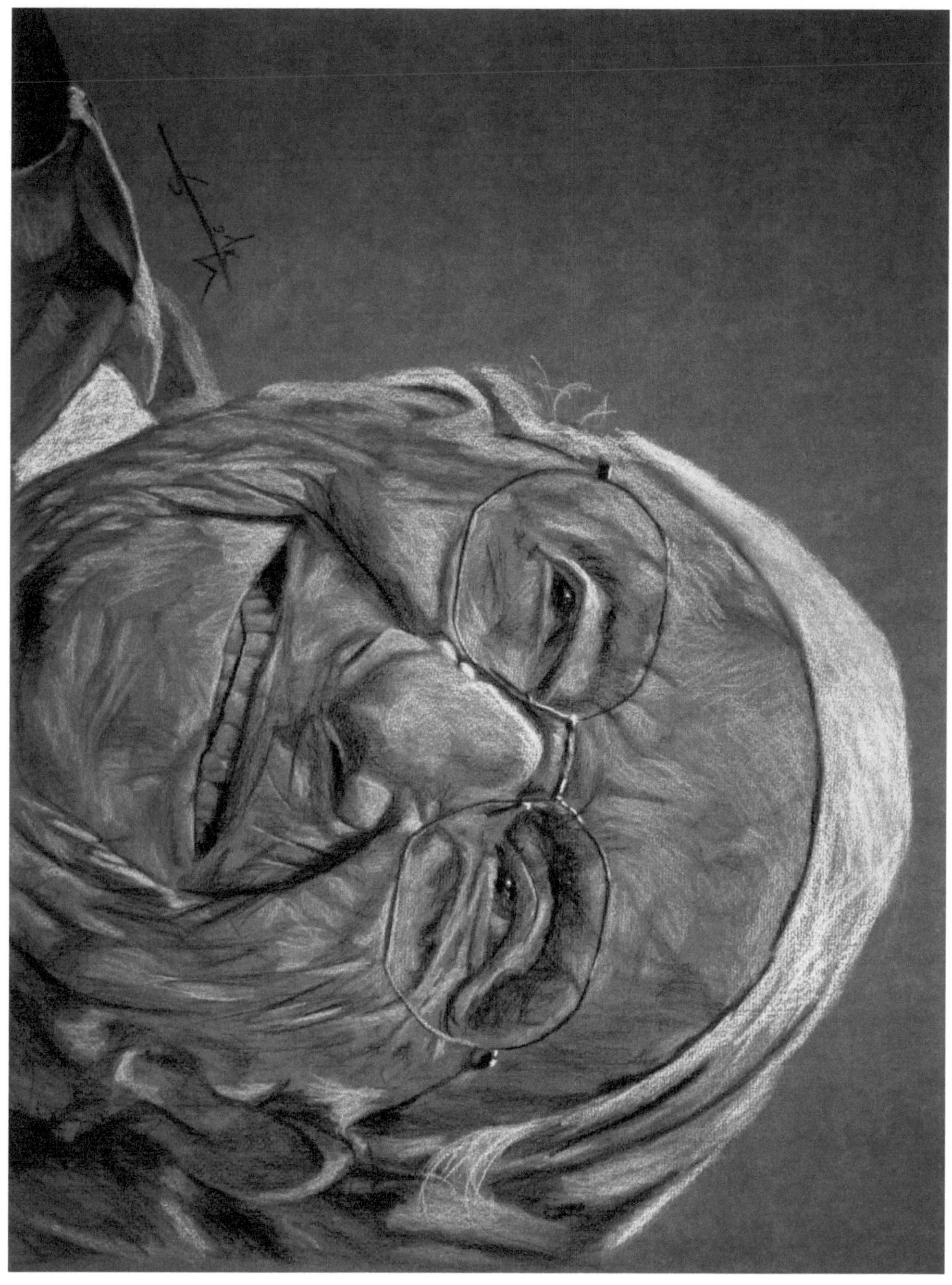

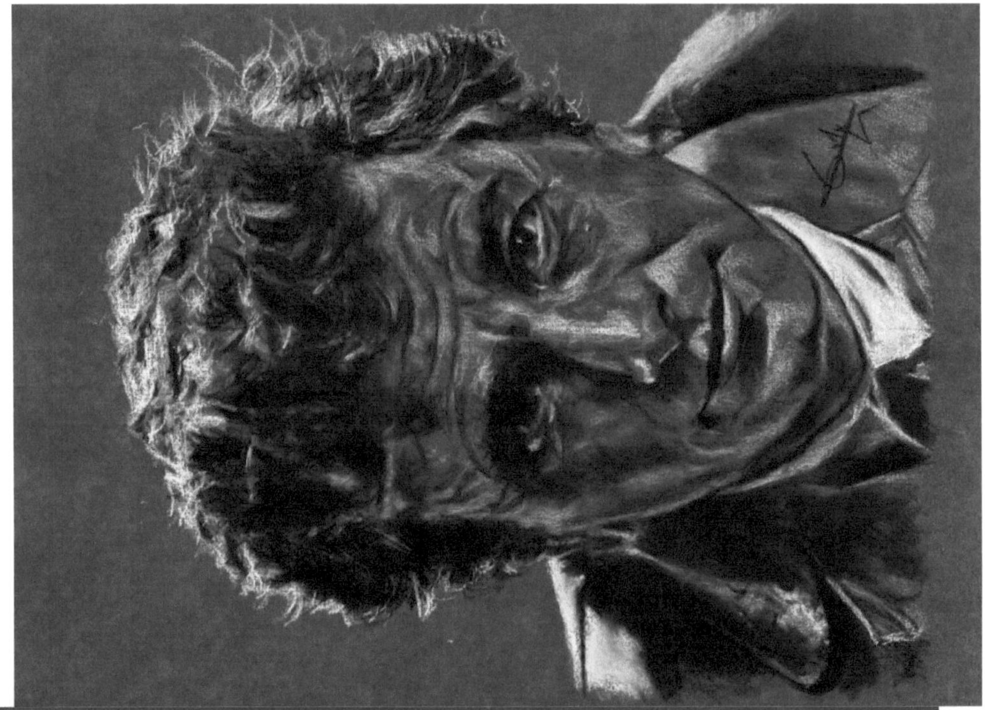

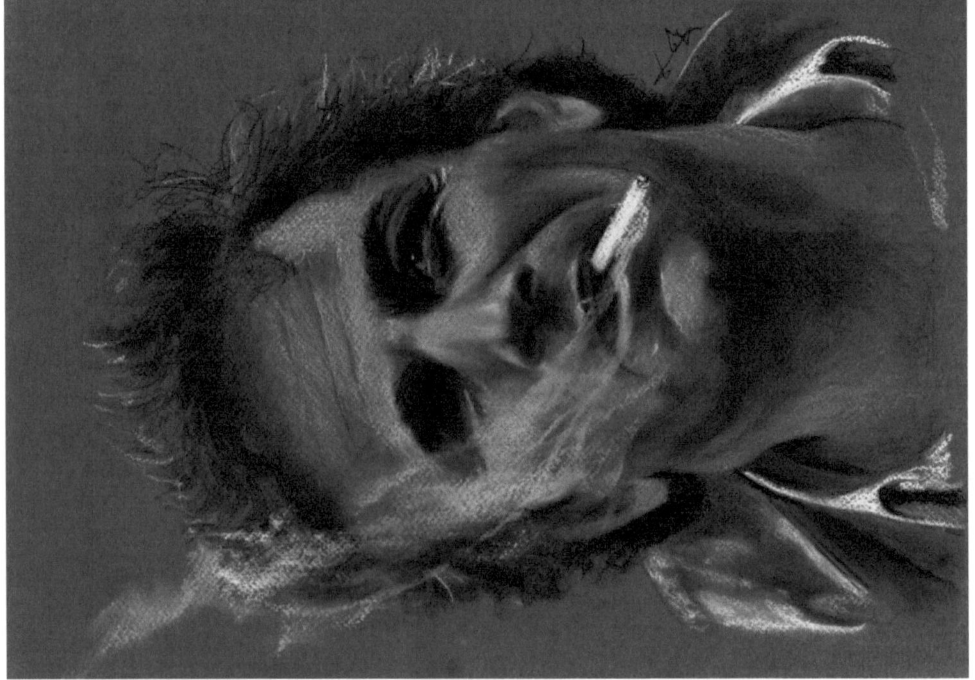

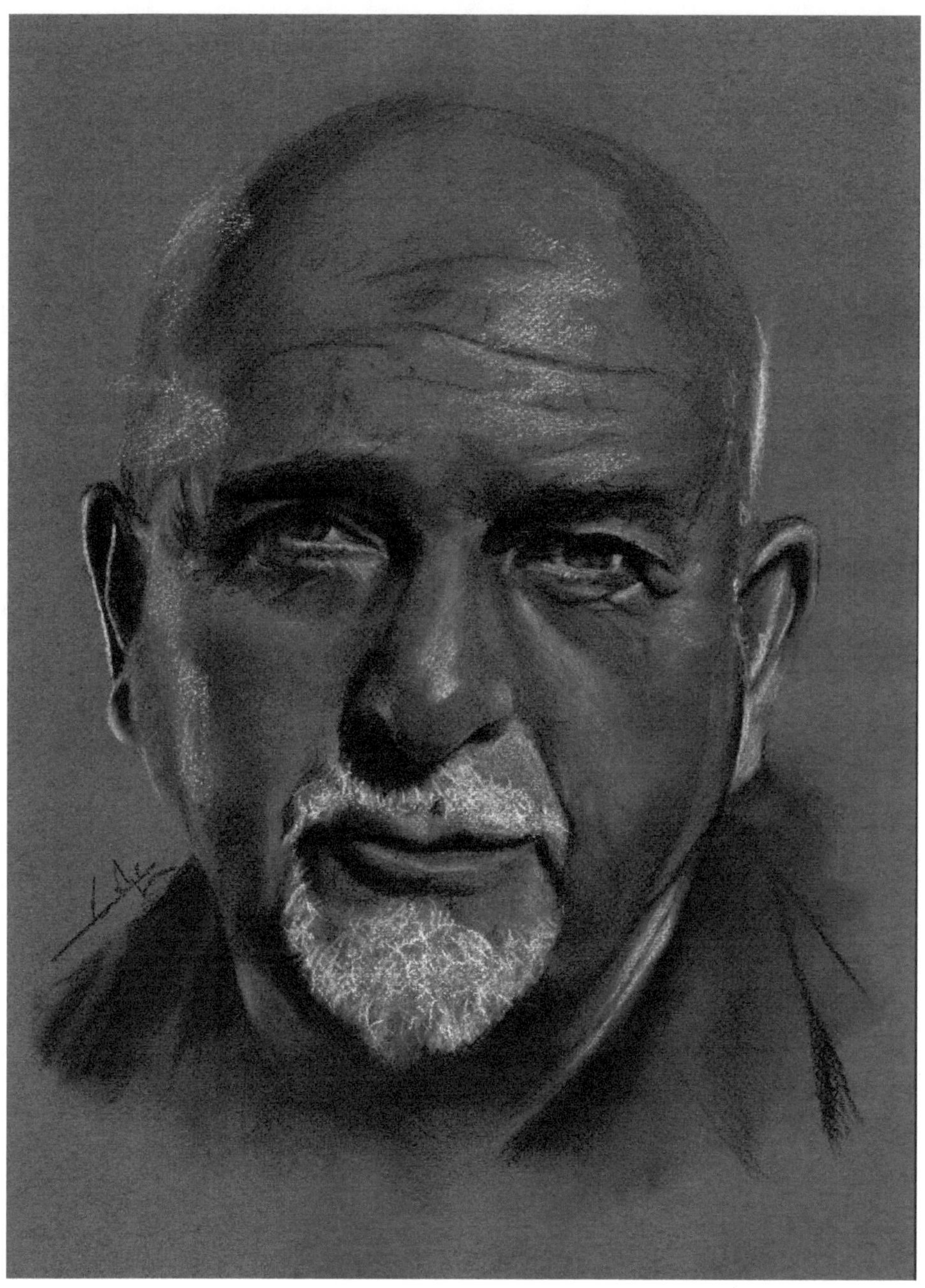

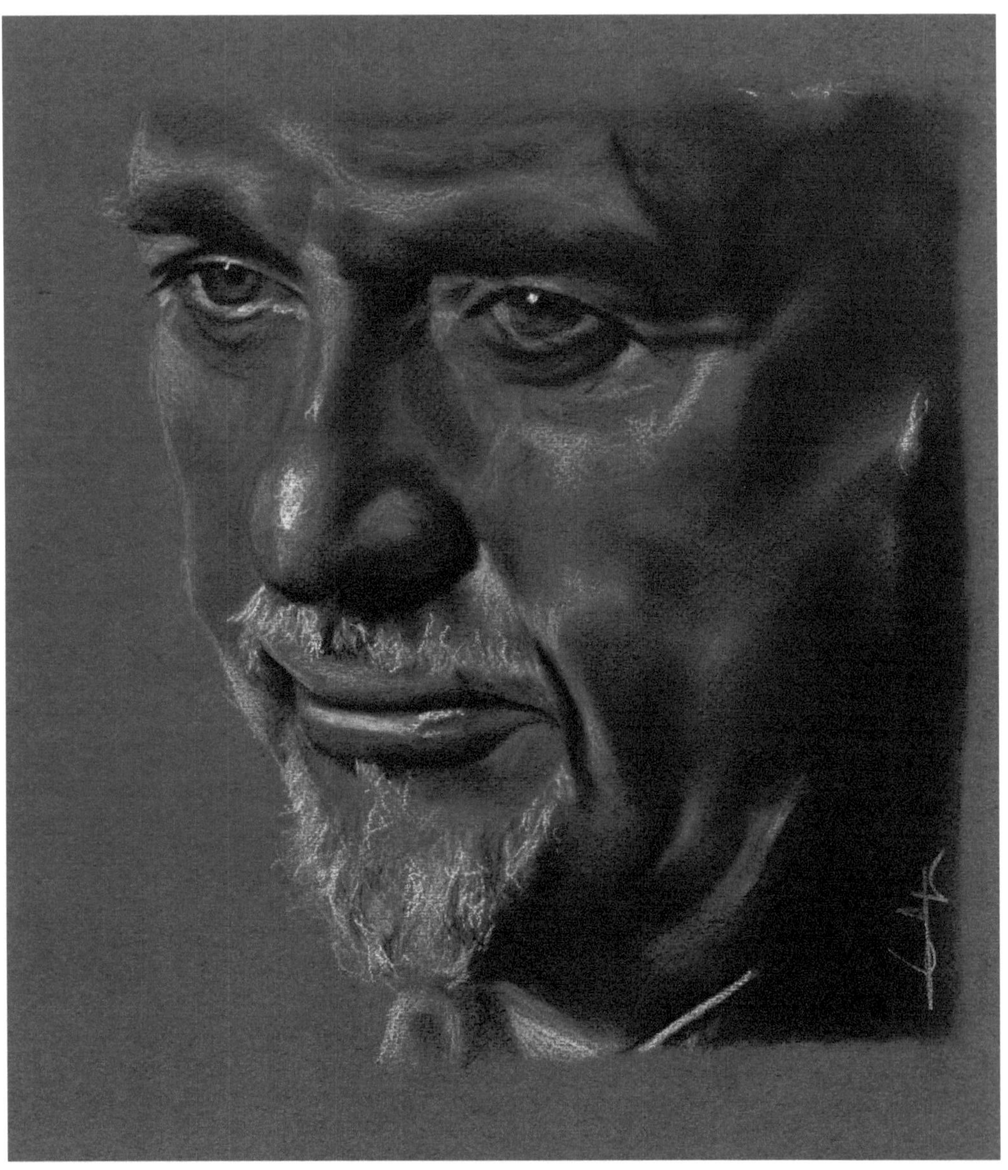

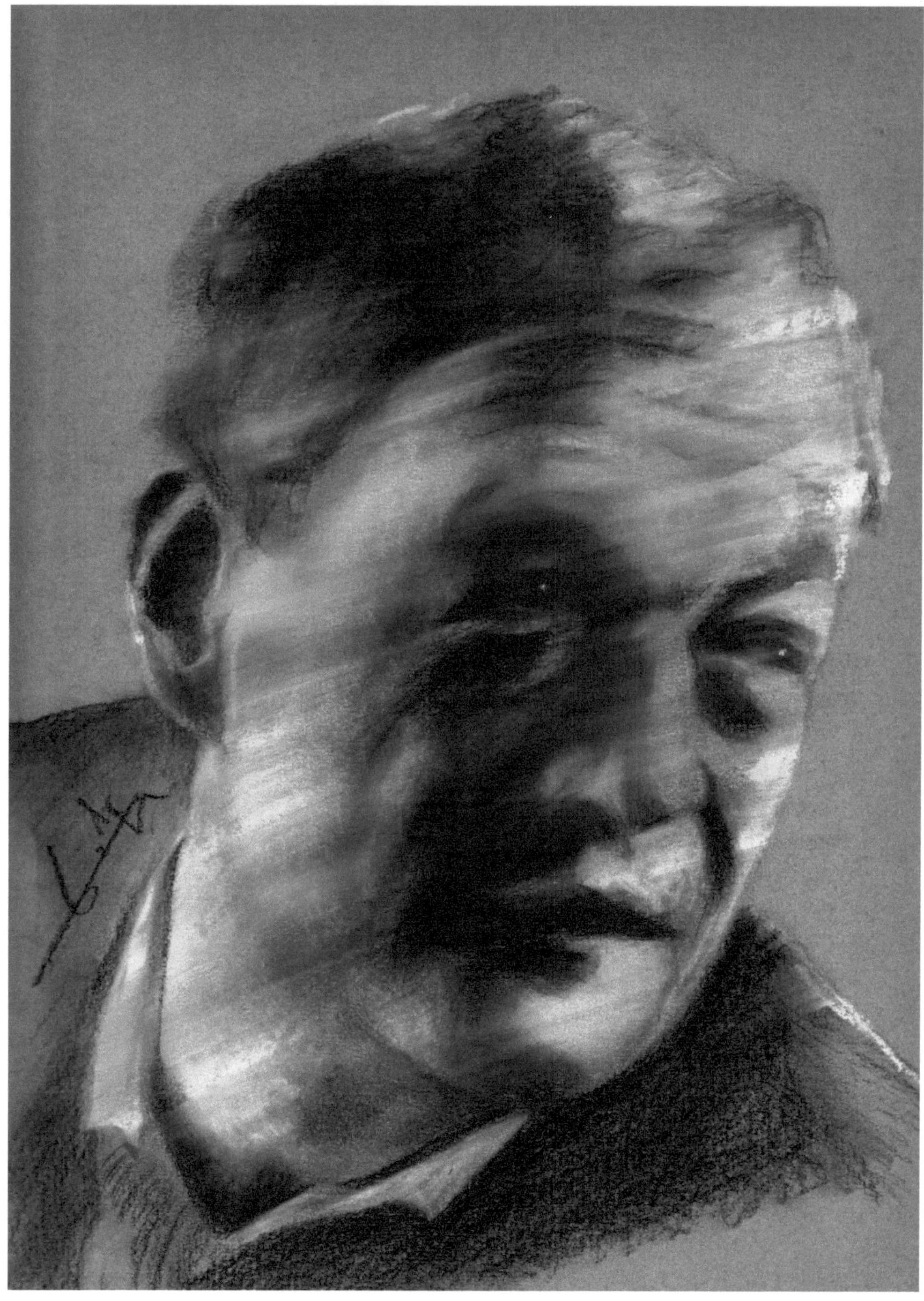

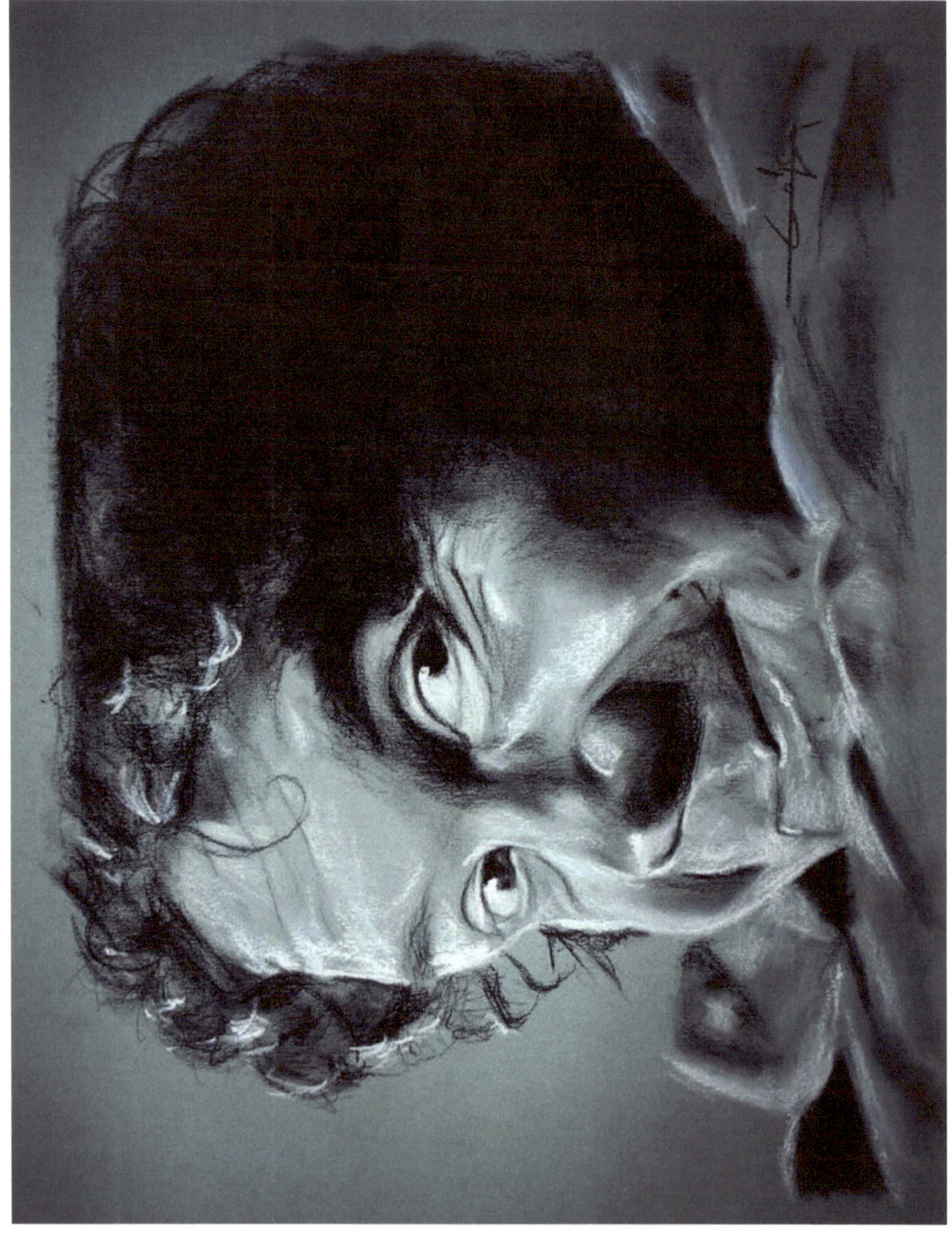

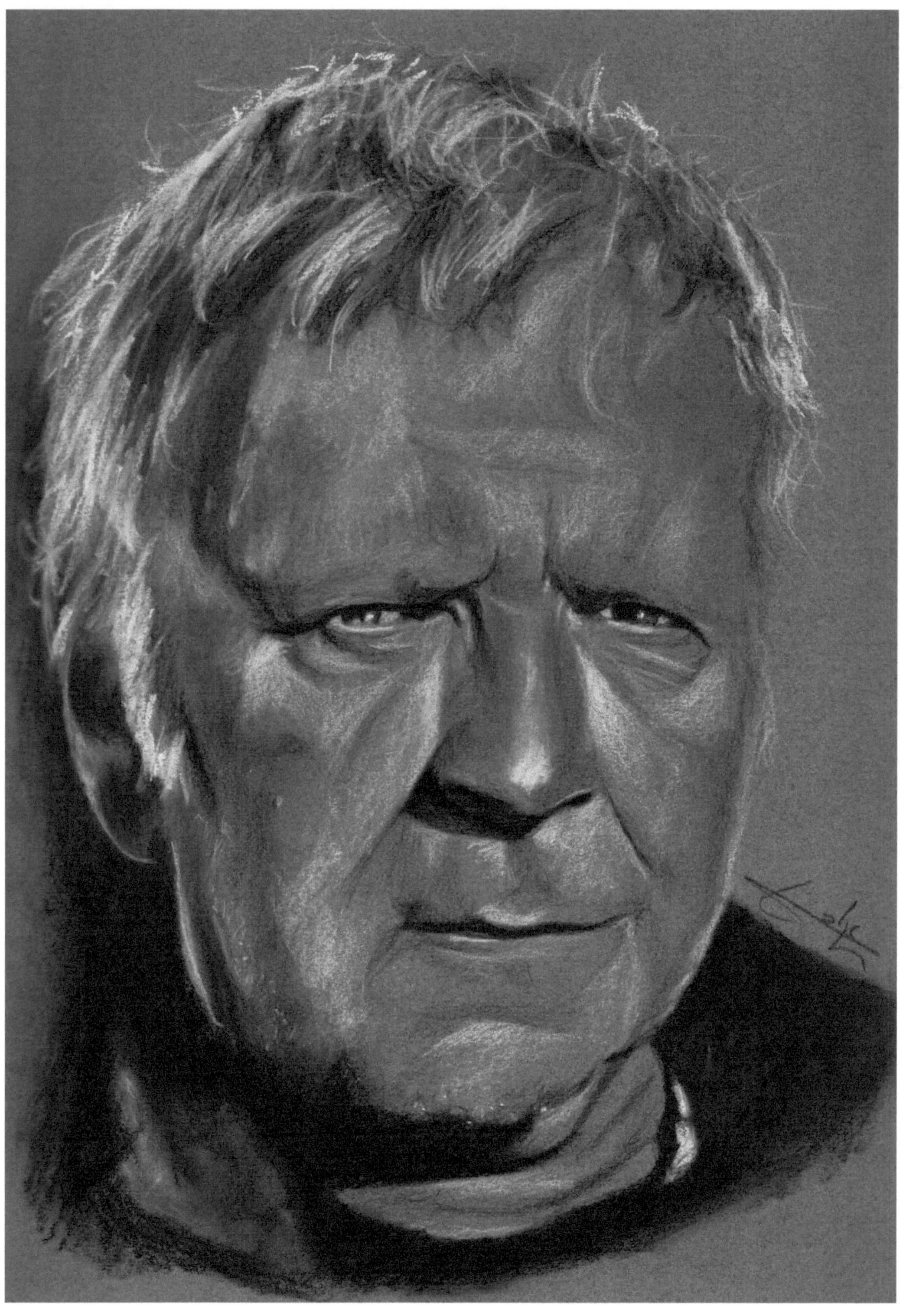

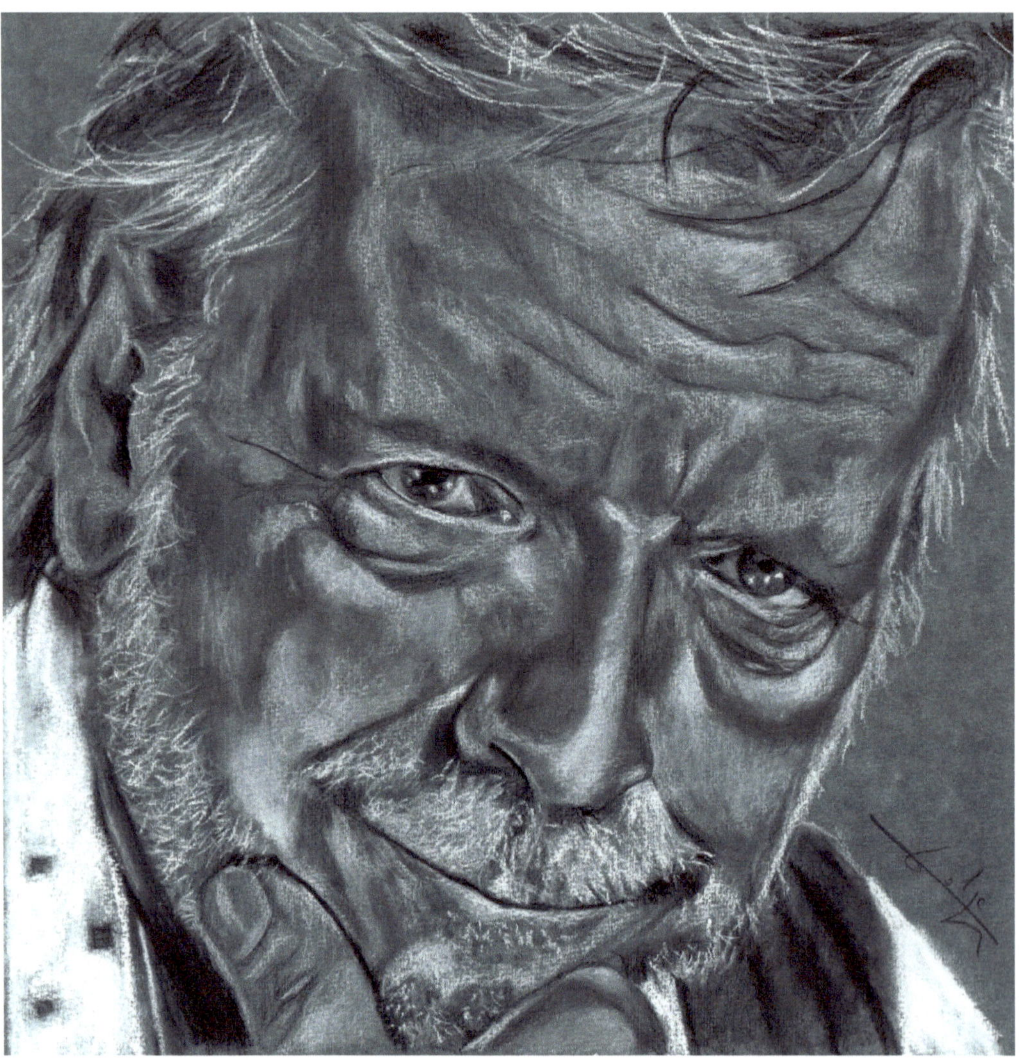

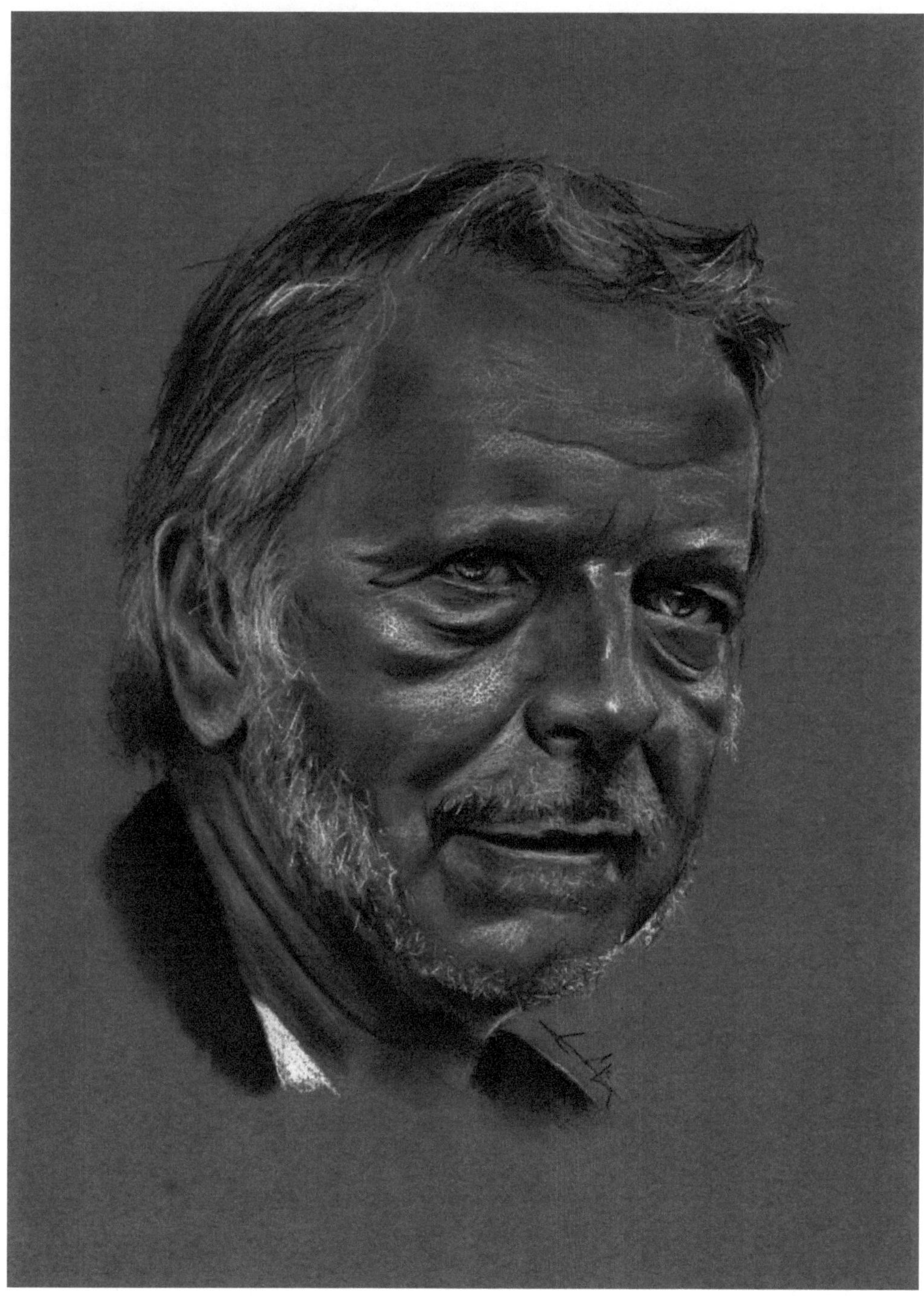

84 Portraits in Chiaroscuro – Philippe Flohic

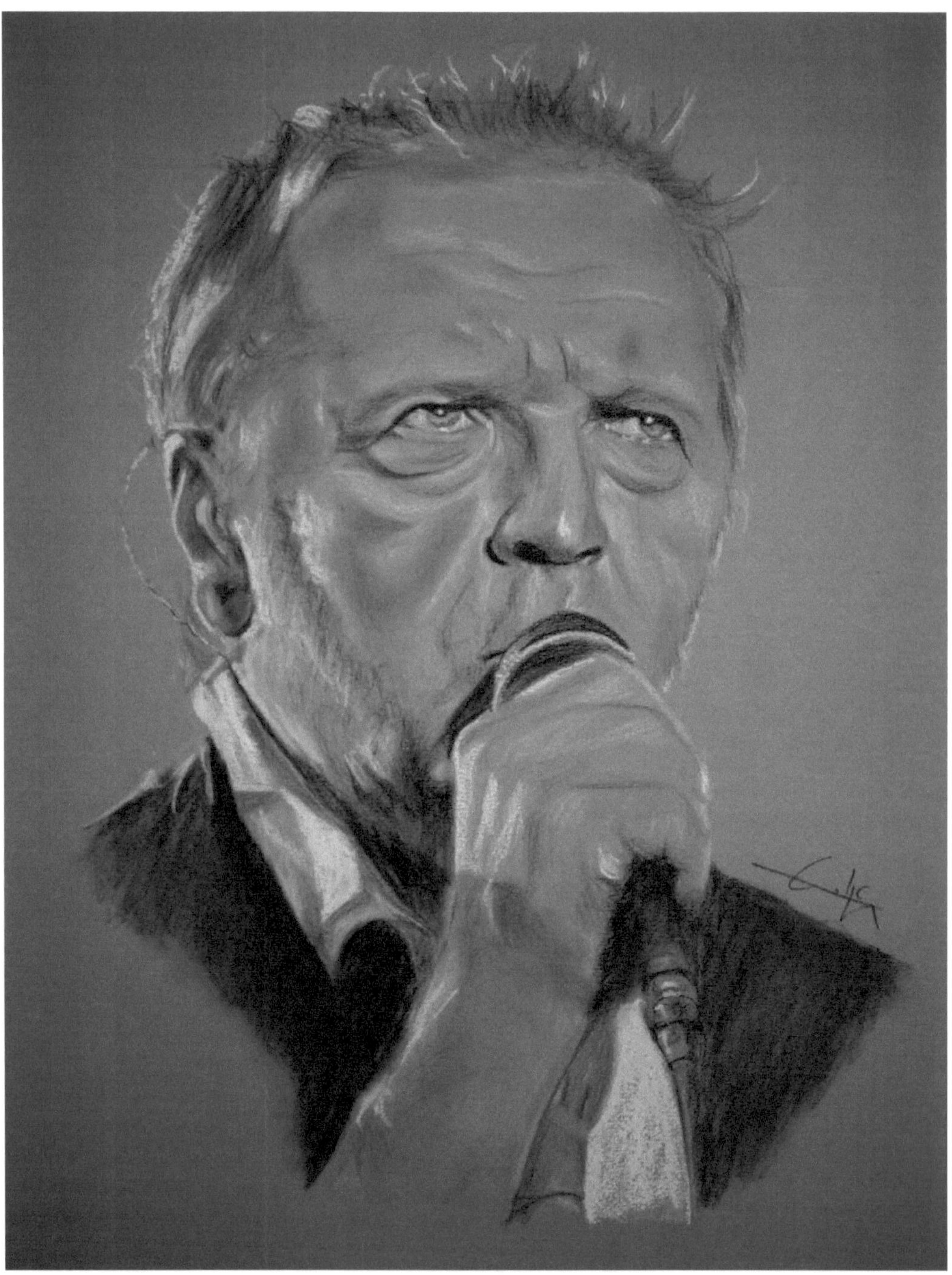

75

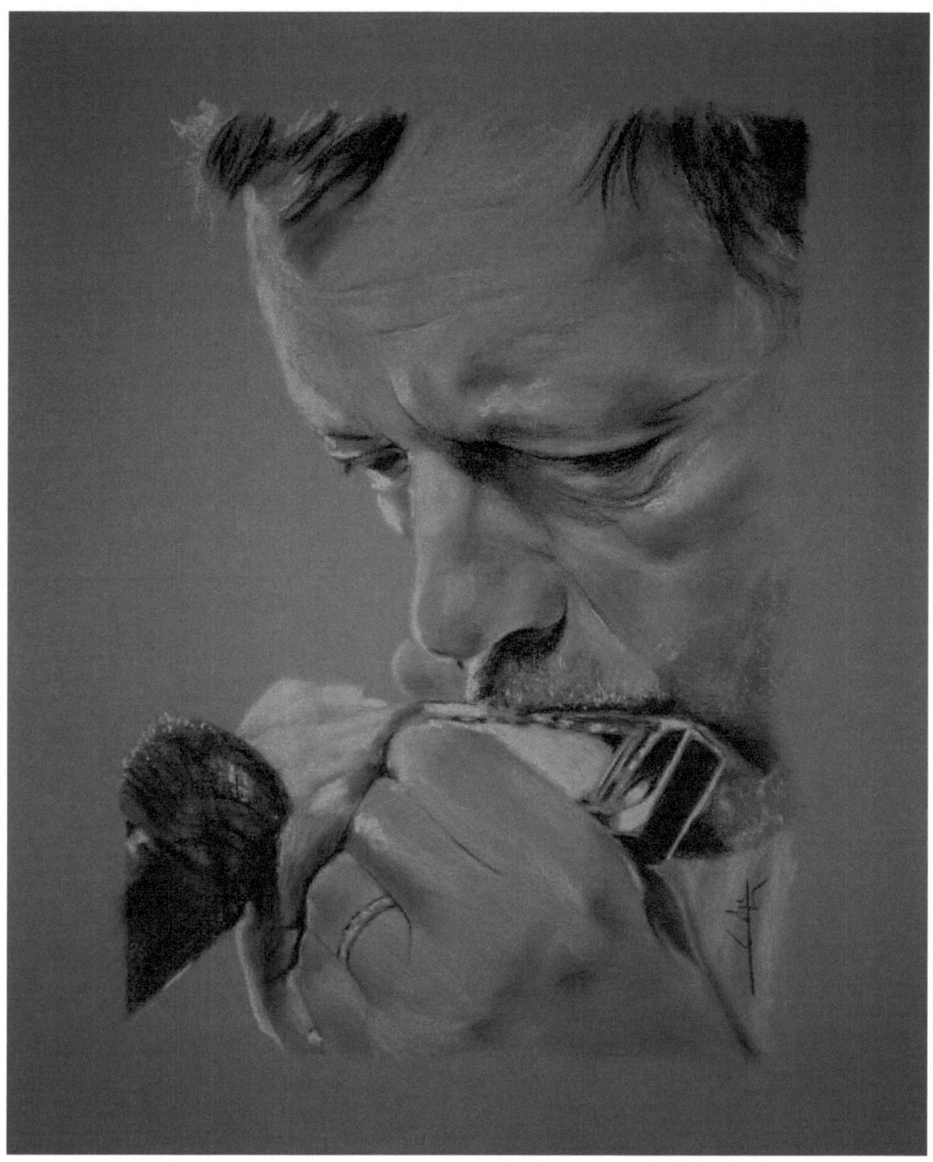

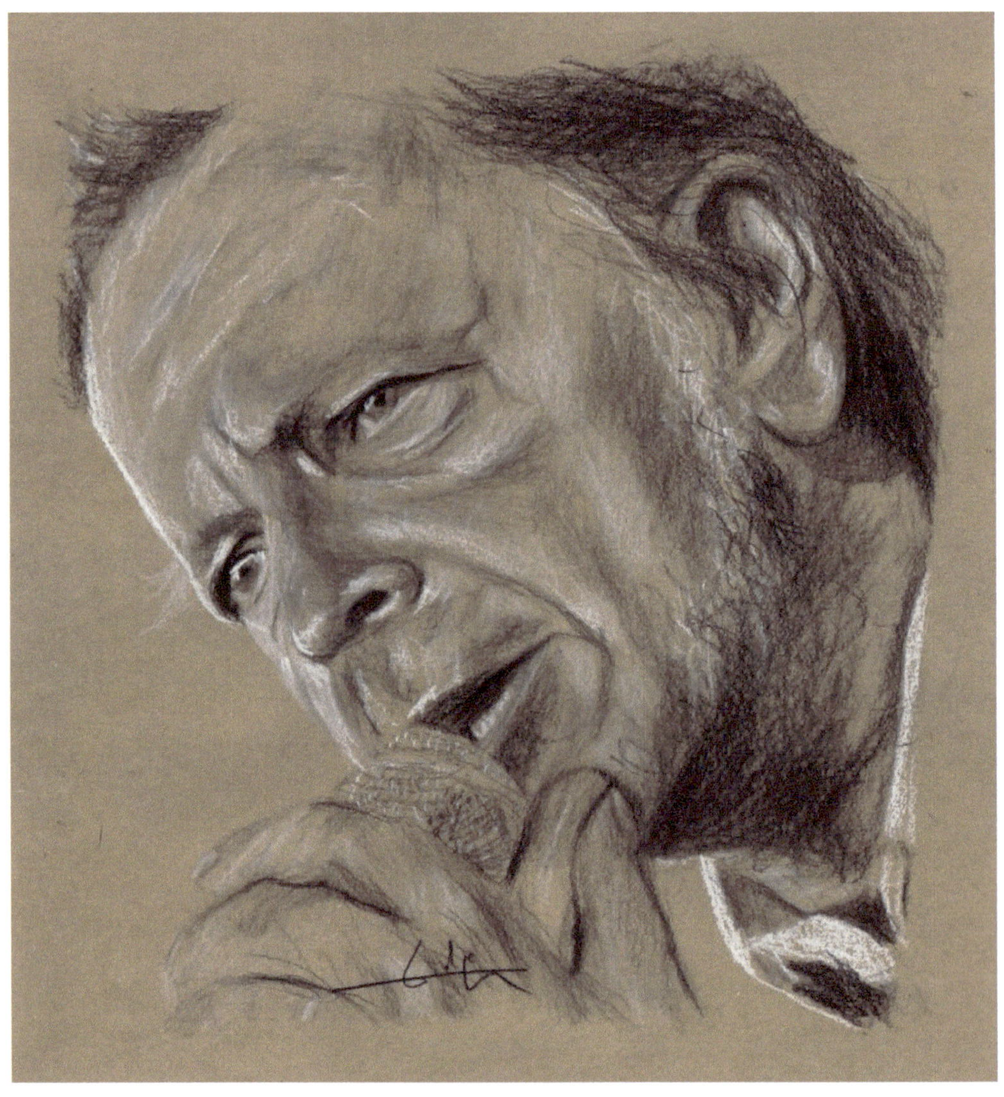

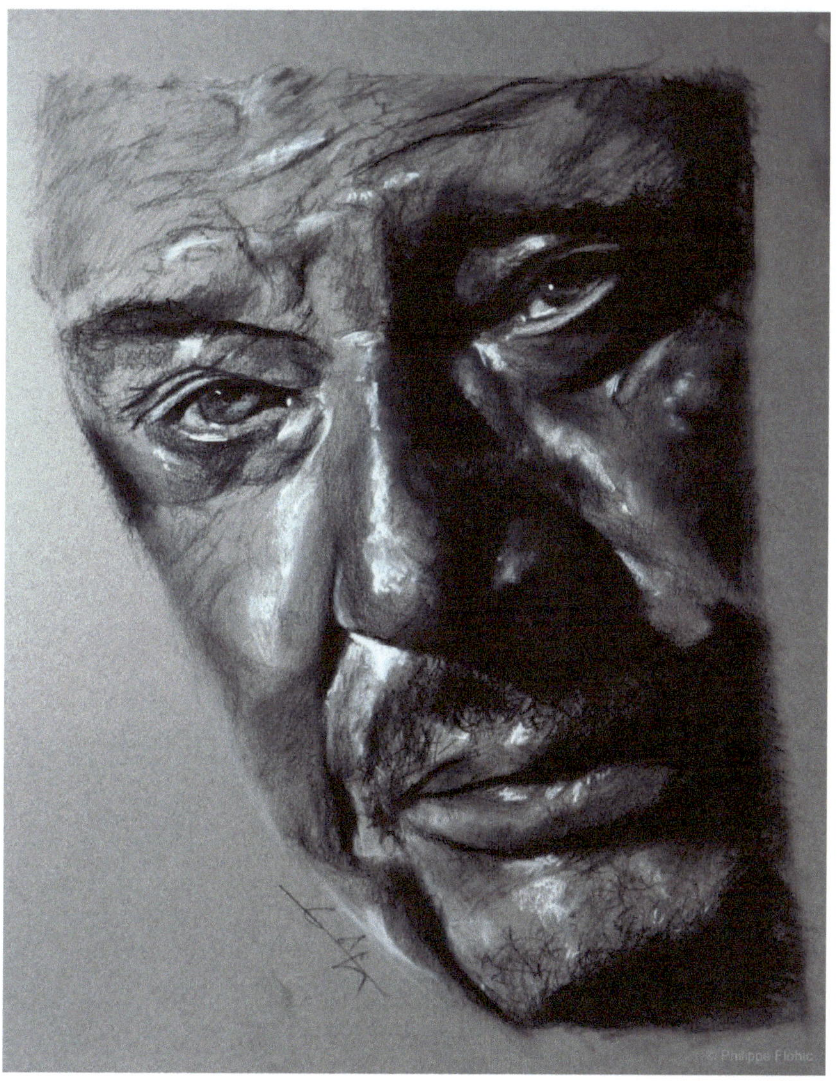

ABOUT THE AUTHOR

Hello, my name is Philippe Flohic. I am 56 years old, in a relationship, and have two grown sons.

For over twenty years, I have been working as a childminder in the north of Toulouse (a large city in the southwest of France). Thanks to this job, I rediscovered my passion for drawing and invested myself in this practice. While some people entertain themselves by watching series or reading, I preferred to pick up my pencils to dedicate myself to making portraits, a theme that has always attracted me.

Over the years, I have perfected my skills in this field, which now allows me to fully flourish and pass on my knowledge to my students.

My mission as an artist and teacher is to offer a simple and playful approach to portrait drawing with chiaroscuro to my students. My goal is to show them that drawing can be fun, accessible, and without constraint. I also want to help them to overcome any complex about academic dogmas on drawing and the structural establishment of the human head.

I am convinced that everyone can draw, regardless of their level of skill or artistic background. With my knowledge and expertise, I am here to help my students unleash their creativity and develop their own drawing style.

I am here to guide my students through each step of the drawing process, from creating outlines to highlighting chiaroscuro. I am here to encourage them to explore their own creativity and express their unique artistic vision.

I am delighted to put my expertise at the disposal of my students and help them develop their passion for drawing. My goal is to create a welcoming and positive atmosphere for learning and artistic expression, where everyone can flourish and find their way in the wonderful world of art.

In short, my mission is to make drawing accessible to all, to give students the confidence to explore their creativity, and to help them discover their own artistic style.

I have been practicing drawing for over 20 years, and over the years, I have explored different methods and techniques to perfect my art. The use of the grid method and a LED projector allowed me to obtain precise proportions and amazing results in creating my first portraits. The use of charcoal and red chalk did the rest of the work, and I was satisfied with my achievements.

However, after using these two aids for some time, I began to tire and look for something new to stimulate me artistically. That's when I discovered chiaroscuro drawing, and it was love at first sight for me. I read and watched a lot of content on this approach to drawing and quickly began applying it to my own portraits.

Since then, I mainly practice this approach to drawing for my portraits. It is an exciting and creative method that allows me to explore different shades of light and shadow to create realistic and expressive portraits. I now feel legitimate to transmit to my students my uncomplexed method to approach the portrait drawing with chiaroscuro in a fun and ludic way.

I am convinced that everyone can learn this technique and make it their own to create unique and personal works. I am excited to share my passion and help you discover this fascinating approach to portrait drawing with chiaroscuro.

https://www.formations-dessin-au-clair-obscur.fr